Stakeholder-oriented Project Management

Tools and Concepts

Research in Design Series

Volume 6

Previously published in this series:

Volume 5
E. Bohemia, K. Harman and K. Lauche
The Global Studio: Linking Research, Teaching and Learning

Volume 4
K. Moraes Zarzar and A. Guney (Eds.)
Understanding Meaningful Environments: Architectural Precedents and the Question of Identity in Creative Design

Volume 3
M. Eekhout and T. Tomiyama (Eds.)
Delft Science in Design 2

Volume 2
E. van de Kar and A. Verbraeck
Designing Mobile Service Systems

Volume 1
R. Binnekamp, L.A. van Gunsteren and P.P. van Loon
Open Design, a Stakeholder-oriented Approach in Architecture, Urban Planning, and Project Management

ISSN 1569-7258 (print)
ISSN 1879-8233 (online)

Stakeholder-oriented Project Management

Tools and Concepts

Lex A. van Gunsteren

in collaboration with:

Ruud Binnekamp
Rein P. de Graaf

Chair of Computer Aided Design and Planning
Faculty of Architecture
Delft University of Technology

IOS Press

ISBN 978-1-60750-700-0 (print)
ISBN 978-1-60750-701-7 (online)

Cover design: Geert Hermkens
Author's photograph: Hans Schouten, Faculty of Architecture, Delft University of Technology

Published and distributed by IOS Press under the imprint Delft University Press

Publisher & Distributor
IOS Press
Nieuwe Hemweg 6b
1013 BG Amsterdam
Netherlands
fax: +31-20-687 0019
email: info@iospress.nl
www.iospress.nl
www.dupress.nl

Distributor in the USA and Canada
IOS Press, Inc.
4502 Rachael Manor Drive
Fairfax, VA 22032
USA
fax: +1-703-323 3668
email: sales@iospress.com
www.iospress.com

PRINTED IN THE NETHERLANDS

Foreword

To practitioners

What is the key to successful management of large and complex construction projects? According to the author: A stakeholder-oriented approach to all issues that may arise. That requires a genuinely stakeholder-oriented mindset ingrained into the culture of the organisation. Norms and values making up that culture tend to be established by the founders of the corporation. The stakeholder-oriented culture of Boskalis has its origin from the very first years of its existence, as was observed by one of the author's students who wrote his master thesis about the history of Boskalis. Likewise, the author and his brother seem to have been highly influenced by the way of conducting business of their own family. Practitioners less privileged with an entrepreneurial upbringing can develop a stakeholder-oriented mindset by reading and reflecting about it. To all of them who wish to broaden their horizon on the art of managing large and complex construction projects, I warmly recommend this book.

Hans Kraaijeveld van Hemert
President (retired), Royal Boskalis Westminster Group

To academics

The new tools and concepts offered in this book on successful project management are interesting for academics in business administration, who teach and research the management of large and complex projects. The stakeholder concept was introduced in the field of strategy a long time ago, but the use of it in managing large scale projects is new. This book gives a solid basis for this new use. The book deals not only with quantitative tools of computer modelling, multi-criteria decision making and probabilistic network planning, but also with qualitative concepts on quality, information handling and the use of power. These concepts and therefore this book deserve to be incorporated into the programs of all leading business schools concerned with large scale international contracting.

Prof. Dr Ir Jaap de Smit
Founder and first dean of the Rotterdam School of Management

Preface

The purpose of this book is two-fold:

1. To serve the needs of students of our course 'Open Design and Construction Management: an Operations Research approach' at Delft University of Technology.

2. To make practitioners familiar with an approach towards project management which is different from but complementary to the current main stream of literature on the subject.

Students have always been a major stimulus for me and have shaped my view that the best of them are essential for the acceptance of any new concepts in practice. Not immediately after their graduation, but after the years they need to acquire the power in their organization to overcome the inevitable fear of innovation.

Practitioners with an open mind to new ideas tend to wrestle with the issue of finding the time to explore those ideas and incorporate them in their daily work. For this reason, we have tried to be concise rather than exhaustive.

Mathematical modeling can be useful for the implementation of best management practices. In regard to project management in particular: network planning and multi-criteria decision making (Chapters 4 and 5). Any feedback from readers on the use of these tools will be highly appreciated.

There are several roads that lead to Rome. Likewise, there are several ways to manage a project. The stakeholder-oriented approach described here deserves to be at least taken into consideration as an alternative to the prevailing control-oriented practice.

Acknowledgements

The following contributions are gratefully acknowledged:

- The experiences with stakeholder-oriented project management that my brother Frans shared with our research group have deepened our views on the subject. His remarks on the poor usefulness of all current planning models has led to the creation of planning software that enables mitigations to be taken into account.
- My collaborators Rein de Graaf and Ruud Binnekamp contributed significantly to Chapter 4 and 5 respectively. Ruud also provided valuable assistance in editing.
- Our students Felipe Castro Arenas and Matthijs Kluis delivered the first case for the appendices and Nikki Oude Elferink wrote the second.
- Jeroen Burger provided valuable assistance in polishing the English and the figures.

Contents

1 Introduction

Complex construction projects seem inevitably to suffer from overruns in time and money and in many cases also disappointing functionality.

> Example: *Amsterdam's North-South metro line*
>
> Figure 1.1 shows how over seven years the North-South metro line project in Amsterdam became twice as expensive and incurred a delay of six years.
>
> The tunneling is still problematic. Monumental houses from the seventeenth century are being irreparably damaged as a result of their foundations being undermined. The end of trouble is still not in sight.

Numerous other examples could be given. Satisfactory completion of large complex construction projects on time and within budget seems to be almost impossible. Nevertheless, it has been proven in practice that large complex projects can be completed with satisfactory quality and within financial and time constraints, although such cases are the exception rather than the rule.

In earlier work (Binnekamp et al., 2006, pp. 99-199), the distinction was made between best management practices for straightforward and predictable projects, labeled PI practices, and best practices for complex and unpredictable projects, called PII practices. The main stream of the literature on project management is about PI management. To validate the view that for complex projects involving a lot of uncertainty PII management practices are required, two cases from practice were investigated in which the project leader had intuitively displayed a PII managerial approach:

Figure 1.1 Amsterdam North-South metro line prognoses of costs and completion date (source: Algemeen Dagblad, December 16, 2009).

1. The US$ 0.6 billion petrochemical process plant for the joint venture between Shell and Mitsubishi on the Seraya Island in Singapore, which was designed and constructed in the period 1990-1997 (Figure 1.2). Frans van Gunsteren (my brother) was, from 1992 onwards, the project manager.

2. 'De Resident', a city-center renovation project in The Hague, close to the Central Station, which was designed and constructed in the period 1989-1998 (Figure 1.3). 'Rijksbouwmeester' Kees Rijnboutt was the project leader.

Frans actually served on two large construction projects in the Far East:

1. The Seraya project mentioned above. Commissioning and successful start-up took place in May 1997 without any overruns in time or money.

2. A Shell-CNOOC petrochemical plant, known as the Shell Nanhai project, in the Guangdong Provence of P.R. China (Frans being involved from 2001). Successful start-up of this US$ 4.3 billion project took place in early 2006 without any overruns in time or money.

Frans, who had left Shell after the Seraya project, had serious doubts when he was invited to come on board again as construction director for the Nanhai project. The risks were so high that he considered the task as almost impossible for anybody. I told him: if Shell's top management sees you as their best option, it is their responsibility, not yours. Yours is to do whatever you can to make it a success regardless what the end result will be. As the Seraya project has been extensively described in Binnekamp et al. (2006), we discuss here only the relevant similarities and differences of the two projects.

Similarities of the projects Seraya and Nanhai

The managerial approach of the Seraya project was also followed in the Nanhai project. This approach can be characterised as follows:

- Start with establishing the overall objectives of the project, based on the stakeholders' long term objectives.

- Identify key issues for important problem areas that are unique for the project concerned.

- Compile a key issue matrix of problem areas (issues) and management tools to address the identified issues.

- Apply PII best management practices where appropriate.

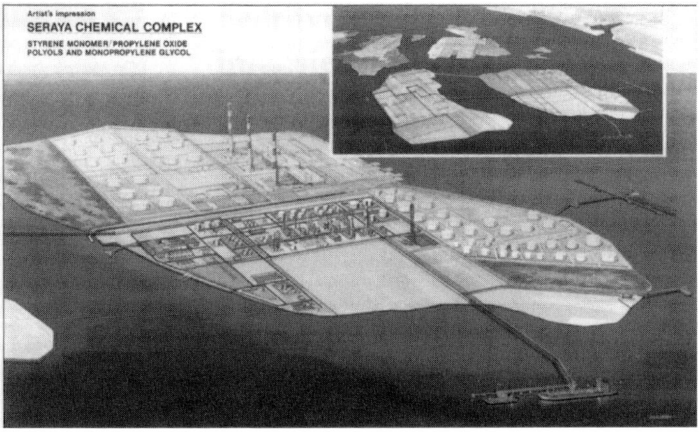

Figure 1.2 An aerial view of Seraya Chemical complex (Shell Venster, 1994, p.21)

Figure 1.3 'De Resident' (Van Rossem, 1996, p. 74)

The resulting key issue matrix for the Nanhai project is given in Table 1.1. The boxes 1.1, 1.2, etc. of the matrix were systematically filled in and translated into concrete managerial actions (of which a description would be beyond the scope of this book).

Differences of the projects Seraya and Nanhai

In hindsight two fundamental differences between the Seraya and Nanhai projects can be identified:

1. Size;
2. Degree of uncertainty.

The *size* of the Nanhai project was enormous, which brings along that the project had to be subdivided into manageable sub-projects, referred to as 'silos'. The coordination of the eleven silos constituted a major planning problem.

The *degree of uncertainty* was relatively low in the Seraya project. There were risks as addressed by the key issue matrix, but few *unknown* dangers. The environment was stable and known from experience. In the Nanhai project, by contrast, the environment was both to a large extent unknown and changing rapidly during the construction phase. The unknown and rapidly changing environment brought along unforeseen issues on-the-run which could not have been anticipated by means of the key issue matrix. Among the issues which arose:

- Overheating of Chinese economy in 2004 resulting in:
  - material cost increase (50%)
  - labor cost increase (average 30%, welders 100%)
  - Shop Loading (some jobs 6 months late)
  - power and water shortage
- Changing rate of exchange
- SARS epidemic and typhoon in 2003
- Sinopec Design Office and Construction Contractors overloaded in 2003, 2004, 2005
- Crude oil price increase in 2005, hurting commissioning budget

How could these issues be addressed? Basically by *a redundancy of capable people and other resources*. All these unforseen issues required a PII approach to resolve them. A comparison of the application of PI and PII practices for the Seraya and Nanhai projects is shown in Table 1.2.

Table 1.1 Resulting Key Issue Matrix Nanhai

Management Tools:	1. Leadership	2. Human resources	3. Open to non-conformance	4. Communication	5. Lessons learned	6. Control
Key Issues:						
1. Project management for new company in green field	1.1	2.1	3.1	4.1	5.1	6.1
2. Huizhou DB infrastructure and experience with petro-chem industry	1.2	2.2	3.2	4.2	5.2	6.2
3. Chinese EPC methods	1.3	2.3	3.3	4.3	5.3	6.3
4. Mindset and language	1.4	2.4	3.4	4.4	5.4	6.4
5. Technology	1.5	2.5	3.5	4.5	5.5	6.5
6. Size	1.6	2.6	3.6	4.6	5.6	6.6

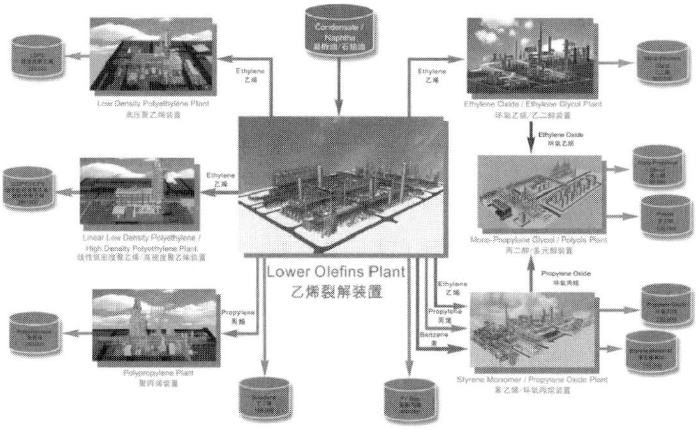

Figure 1.4 Nanhai project divided into eleven 'silos'

Table 1.2 Application of best practices in Seraya and Nanhai

Seraya	Nanhai
Aspect:	
1. Goal setting – fixed vs. floating	
The strategic scope and set up of the project was set and fixed according PI practices.	The strategic scope was according PI practices, the implementation according PII practices, especially in 2005, prior to start up.
2. Leadership – boss focused vs. stakeholder focused	
Mutual support played the important role and non-manipulative cooperation in a PII manner, to align contractor and owner.	Vulnerable leadership based on PII practices in unknown territory.
3. Conflict resolution – compromise vs. synthesis	
The shareholder alignment was successful according PII practices.	Special risk of joint ventures in china required daily PII approaches.
4. Design process – solution point vs. solution space	
A PII scope, omissions managed on the run (offices).	Outsourcing air separation unit after approval project scope reduction (Rail).
5. Communication – information oriented vs. decision oriented	
Weekly meetings by Arjan and Frans on information needs as PII.	PII weekly metrics/trends plus 'light management' mitigation.
6. Persuasion of players – window dressing vs. valid and relevant information	
A good and open PII approach.	Tried to achieve decisions based on facts (PII) rather than power play (PI).
7. Progress control – hard info oriented vs. soft info oriented	
PI hurdle by construction ignoring metrics, PII recovery by parallel commission & construction.	PII engagement key to 'mood' and hard results: PI Blocks in construction die-hards.
8. Division of tasks – job descriptions vs. roles	
Arjan/Frans working in PII allowed overlapping roles resulting in quick decisions and effective teamwork.	PII the same as in Seraya, and very effective in off-site scope.
9. Co-ordination of tasks – project manager's coordination vs. mutual adjustment	
The same experiences as with Aspect 8.	Owner on board, PMC after two years, contractors never.
10. Standardization – where possible vs. where functional	
PI technical flaw originated from oil standards applied to chemicals; PII solved on the run.	Technical deviation on the run, 2004/2005 PII.

The Nanhai project satisfied all stakeholders' performance criteria:

- HSE — Health very good; Safety acceptable; Environment very good
- Cost — Within budget of feasibility 1997
- Schedule — As planned
- Quality — Above expectation
- Reputation — Pro-actively managed and delivered

The success of the two projects induced our research group to interview Frans in order to establish how this was achieved. Our conclusion (Binnekamp et al., 2006) was that, in addition to a redundancy of capable people and other resources, the style of management of Frans and his team had been of paramount importance. Their approach largely reflected the best practices we have labeled PII, as opposed to PI traditional management practices as generally recommended in the literature on project management.

It appeared that Frans utilized surprisingly few of the techniques that the literature on project management offers and that he deliberately ignored some so-called best practices that are recommended in that literature.

What then guided his behavior that, apparently, led to such successful construction management? Reflecting upon this question, I have come to the conclusion that the essence is: *a stakeholder-oriented approach to all issues that (may) arise**. The interest of *all* stakeholders as a basis for decision-making: experts as well as laymen, powerful ones as well as stakeholders with little influence, Eastern as well as Western stakeholders, etc.

Such a mindset, focused at the interests of all stakeholders, can be in conflict with many best practices recommended in the literature, such as:

- Concentrate on fulfilling the contract. Make sure you comply with its specifications. Frans: 'After signing, the contract does not exist anymore for me as a basis for decision-making.'
- Make a plan and stick to it. Frans: 'Be prepared to adjust your planning every week.'
- Concentrate on activities on the Critical Path. Frans: 'There is no such thing as a Critical Path.'

We will come back on these points, and many more, in this work.

The stakeholder-oriented mindset of Frans originates from our upbringing. Our grandfather founded the inland shipping company Damco in 1918. Fifty-seven years later, when our father retired, its fleet of over 300 ships was almost the largest on the Rhine. An example of their stakeholder-oriented style

*A stakeholder is a party actively involved in the project or whose interests may be affected by the performance or completion of the project.

of management is their policy in regard to insurance issues. Instead of claiming as much money as possible from the insurance company, as would be the thing to do according to PI practices, their policy was to demand from the skippers to avoid collisions where possible and not to claim small damages. The resulting favorable track record of claims enabled our father to negotiate every year with Lloyd's a substantial discount on the premium that had to be paid. Damco's history (from 1905 until 1975) has been described in De Wit and Lentjes (1998). In his foreword, Frans confirms its influence on his thinking: 'I became impressed by the way quality was achieved: carefully, conscientiously, balanced, *with understanding of the role of all involved*.'

If norms and values from one's upbringing are so important, does it make sense to write a book about it for readers who were not blessed with a Calvinistic upbringing like ours? Optimistically, I think it does and hope that practitioners with a feel for what is really required will get from this book just the little push needed to have the guts to follow their intuition.

Tools and concepts offered in this volume can help to bring about the desirable way of managing complex projects. They have proven their value in the practice of Frans, myself, and other practitioners.

2 The stakeholder-oriented mindset

In simple construction projects, management tends to focus not so much on functionality but mainly on how to avoid overruns in time and money. Most of the literature on construction project management addresses this issue, resulting in what are nowadays considered to be the best project management practices for the construction industry. See for instance Gray and Hughes (2001); Kerzner (1998); Ritz (1993); Bennet (1991); Nicholas (2004). In the Dutch literature the most widely used book is *Projectmatig werken* by Wijnen et al. (2007, 1st ed. 1984), as it is used by the country's leading construction management consultant firm as the basis for their consulting. We will now summarize these practices and discuss the limits of their applicability.

2.1 Best practices for managing simple projects

In Tables 2.1, 2.2, and 2.3 we have summarized, in ten aspects, the best practices for project management and their implications as can be found in the literature on the subject. We call them PI practices, for simple projects, which we distinguish from PII practices, being more appropriate for managing complex projects. These PII practices will subsequently be presented and summarised on the same ten aspects.

Limits of applicability of PI practices

In the construction industry, the PI project management practices have indeed been very effective at avoiding overruns in time and money. They were so successful in this domain that, in the eighties and nineties, consulting firms were trying to transfer these practices to the realm of industrial research and development (R&D). Overruns in time and money were a serious problem in that domain as well. The results, however, were disappointing. The R&D scientists involved felt that these practices could not be applied in an R&D environment characterized by uncertainty, complexity, and unpredictability (Van Gunsteren, 2003). For instance, setting goals at the beginning and not changing them during the process is not possible in ambitious, innovative R&D projects (Aspect 1). New insights emerging from the R&D-efforts made so far may give rise to an adjustment of goals and objectives. In addition, dividing the work into small steps with identifiable milestones is often hardly possible or desirable in R&D (Aspect 8). And in R&D, standardization is postponed as much as possible to avoid unnecessary exclusion of new concepts (Aspect 10).

The literature on management of technological innovation offers concepts and recommended practices that are fundamentally different from those on

Table 2.1 Best project management practices, PI: Process related issues

Aspect:	Best practice:	Implications:
1. Goal setting	Before awarding a contract – for design and/or construction – the design brief or the design itself should be frozen and not be unfrozen before commissioning.	• Set goals at the start and do not change them before project completion. • Separate design and construction as rigorously as possible.
2. Leadership	Leadership is provided by the project manager, who is the central figure in the entire process.	• Individual prominence becomes a dominant selection criterion for the project manager (to ensure he or she has sufficient reference power).
3. Conflict resolution	Focus on powerful stakeholders and try to establish compromises between them.	• Define limits of formal and sanction power. • Power structure determines outcome.
4. Design process	Proceed from coarse, preliminary design towards detailed design in a trial-and-error process starting from an arbitrarily chosen first design.	• Focus initially on getting a solution, i.e. a solution point. • Freeze the design or subsystem design when necessary to keep deadlines.

Table 2.2 Best project management practices, PI: Information handling related issues

Aspect:	Best practice:	Implications:
5. Communication	Keep everyone involved informed on design status, approved changes and planning.	• Use bulletin board and Internet to give everyone access to status information. • Communication is information oriented.
6. Persuasion of players	Make presentations to convince players who have to accept compromises.	• Pay attention to PR and image building. • Use powerful audio-visual aids.
7. Progress control	Divide the process into small steps with identifiable milestones against planned deadlines.	• Separate object from process to make it. • Focus on process for project control.

Table 2.3 Best project management practices, PI: Structure related issues

Aspect:	Best practice:	Implications:
8. Division of tasks	Define division of tasks and associated responsibilities in job and function descriptions.	• Control of progress on predetermined tasks. • Responsibility for right information at the right place determined by job description: information push.
9. Integration and coordination of tasks	Integration and coordination of tasks is a prime responsibility of the project manager.	• White spots, unexpected problems, are resolved by the project manager who uses formal and sanction power to do so. • Little reliance on personal initiatives from people involved.
10. Standardization	Standardization where possible, because standardization reduces complexity.	• Trend towards uniformity. • Seasoned project managers tend to reject new concepts that are hard to standardize.

which PI project management practices are based. See, for instance, Blake (1978); Twiss (1992); Van Gunsteren (2003); Mintzberg (1979).

Urban planners made the same observations regarding the project management approach from the construction industry: that it was not applicable in an urban planning environment. This often happened when the actual urban planning problem concerned a new infrastructure development or an inner city redevelopment situation (Van Loon, 1998). Due to the technical complexity of these kinds of problems, engineers from the construction industry became dominant in these planning processes. At the start of such processes they came with already completed designs for the infrastructure and the buildings to be realized (Aspect 1). Their attention was on the persuasion of the decision makers for their well-worked-out ideas (Aspect 6).

For urban planners, it was hard to fit these proposals into their broader planning issues such as social welfare in the city, economic improvement of the urban area, and social justice in housing distribution. There was no real solution space in these designs for combinations with the objectives of other stakeholders than the construction firms and the real estate owners (Aspect 4).

Table 2.4 Best practices (PII) of Open Design and Construct Management: Process related issues

Aspect:	Best practice:	Implications:
1. Goal setting	Nothing is fixed in advance; be prepared to adjust goals when circumstances change and insight improves.	• Re-evaluation of project objectives at regular intervals. • Adjustment of goals and deadlines according to new insight.
2. Leadership	Aim at leadership focused at defending relevant stakeholders' interests.	• Give project management authority to make connections to all stakeholders. • Select non-manipulative person as project manager.
3. Conflict resolution	Aim at open synthesis (not closed compromise), i.e. choices aimed at satisfaction of stakeholders concerned.	• Equal treatment of powerful and less powerful stakeholders and of experts and laymen. • Valid information rather than power structure determines outcome.
4. Design process	Proceed from ideal constraints of stakeholders to alleviated constraints to achieve a solution at all.	• Think in terms of solution space, not solution point. • Respect constraint ownership; no change without stakeholder consent.

2.2 Best practices for managing complex projects

In Tables 2.4, 2.5, 2.6 we summarize the best practices for managing complex projects as can be derived from R&D management practice (Van Gunsteren, 2003) and from Open Design methodology (Van Loon, 1998; Van Gunsteren and Van Loon, 2000). We call these PII best practices for complex projects.

Limits of applicability of PII practices

Adoption of PII practices is not necessary, and even undesirable, in projects that are not characterized by uncertainty, unpredictability, and a multitude of stakeholders with conflicting interests. It should be emphasized that complex projects can often be subdivided into smaller sub-projects that are relatively straightforward. Application of PII practices should then be limited to the overall project, whilst managing the straightforward sub-projects according to traditional PI project management practices, as summarized earlier.

The project manager will largely take care of the management of the overall

Table 2.5 Best practices (PII) of Open Design and Construct Management: Information handling related issues

Aspect:	Best practice:	Implications:
5. Communication	Respond to information needs and demands of decision-makers (designers, stakeholders).	• Be open in communication; provide valid info to whoever needs it. • Be honest about slacks and margins, i.e. the solution space. • Communication is decision oriented.
6. Persuasion of players	Persuade by supplying valid and relevant information.	• No hidden agenda or window dressing. • Accept consequences of being honest no matter how painful these may be.
7. Progress control	Pay attention to both 'hard' and 'soft' information on progress.	• Pay equal attention to formal and informal information to anticipate pro-actively. • Value and appreciate initiatives from players to warn in time for forthcoming disasters.

Table 2.6 Best practices (PII) of Open Design and Construct Management: Structure related issues

Aspect:	Best practice:	Implications:
8. Division of tasks	Think in roles rather than tasks, using only broad job descriptions.	• Rely on mutual adjustment rather than sharp division of tasks. • Make groups responsible, also for information they need: information pull.
9. Integration and coordination of tasks	Create a climate for mutual adjustment of tasks.	• Allow project manager to delegate part of the coordination tasks to people he or she trusts. • Promote integration of tasks by emphasis on functional performance achieved collectively.
10. Standardization	Standardization only where functional and genuinely accepted by stakeholders.	• Do not push uniformity. • Be, selectively, open to new concepts.

project himself, preferably with a stakeholder-oriented approach, and delegate the management of the sub-projects to others who can manage those in the classical manner. In this way, not everybody involved has to embrace the stakeholder-oriented management style.

A project manager who has a stakeholder-oriented mindset will intuitively apply PII best practices when the situation so requires.

Effective project management is achieved by an appropriate mixture of the application of PI and PII best practices, depending on the situation at hand: straightforward and predictable or complex and unpredictable.

It should be noted that, in addition to the best practices PII of Tables 2.4, 2.5, and 2.6, the following aspects related to the project team were considered to be crucial for success in both the Seraya and the 'Resident' project:

1. Selection of key people;
2. Team building;
3. Commitment to a common cause;
4. Ability to turn problems into opportunities.

This completes our prerequisites for successful implementation of complex construction projects.

3 Objectives, Charter, Project team

Projects have a purpose. An end result which has satisfactory quality as perceived by its sponsor has to be achieved. But what is 'satisfactory quality'? It seems that everyone involved has a different idea of what quality is. As a result, it is often unclear what the objectives of the project are, which makes it impossible to establish its success or failure.

In this chapter, a concept of quality (Van Gunsteren, 2003) is offered which facilitates objectives of the project to be defined. In addition, the concept enables deciding on deviations from specified quality without affecting the overall objectives of the project.

3.1 A quality classification

What is quality?

> Doing or making something well according to the norms of an evaluator or end user.

These norms depend on the purpose one has in mind, hence the definition:

> *Quality is fitness for purpose.*

That means quality is:

1. Related to a subjective purpose.
2. A perception.

Absolute standards of quality do not exist. What quality is depends on the needs of the user. These needs are not only determined by the user's personal desires and preferences, but whenever new technologies offer new possibilities, the wishes of users will also become more demanding. If we wish to get something done from a larger group of people, we have to resort to regulation: laws for a country; rules and standards for a trade; rules, procedures and policies for a corporation. Therefore:

> *Quality is not only a matter of knowledge and mentality, but equally of a proper definition of adequate quality specifications.*

Quality specifications – i.e. norms enabling the measurement of performance in doing or making – depend on:

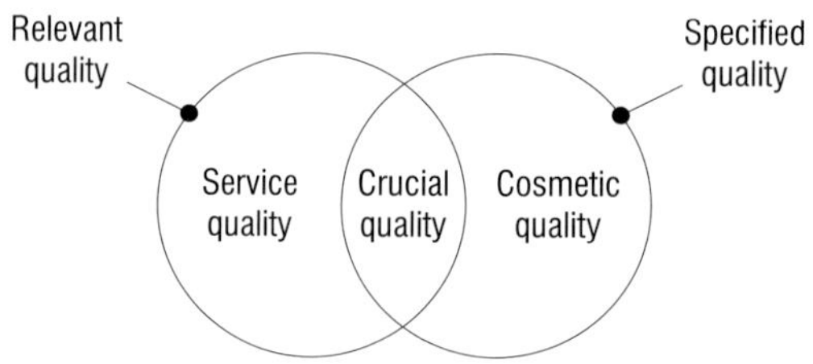

Figure 3.1 Quality specifications never cover exactly all relevant quality.

1. *Purpose* of the end user (clean office, car that does not break down, etc.).
2. Experience in the past as far as *user problems* are concerned.
3. *What can be measured?*

Quality can be:

1. *Relevant* or irrelevant.
2. *Realized* or not realized in the product or service.
3. *Specified* or not included in specifications.

Combinations of these aspects yield seven categories of quality which we will now discuss.

Quality specifications will never cover all quality which is relevant to the end user exactly (Figure 3.1). Relevant quality which is covered by specifications is labeled *crucial quality*, because it is absolutely crucial to realize this type of quality in the product or service. In the case of non-compliance, a claim would be justified both formally and because the user really needs that quality for his purpose. Relevant quality which is not specified is called *service quality*, because this quality has to be delivered as a service if the end user's needs are to be properly satisfied. Specified quality that does not serve any purpose of the end user is labeled *cosmetic quality*. Cosmetic quality consists of:

1. *Ritual quality*: realized cosmetic quality, and
2. *Excuse quality*: non-realized cosmetic quality.

Specifications (standards) are sometimes used as an excuse to exclude a supplier. For instance, the dimensions of car number plates in a certain country were prescribed in such a way that foreign suppliers were handicapped. In

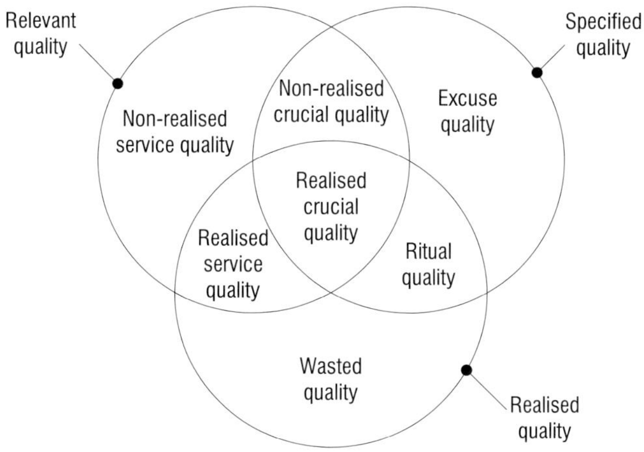

Figure 3.2 Classification of seven categories of quality.

another country, an old-fashioned, inaccurate method to measure the dimensions of marine propellers (using templates) was prescribed to protect the backward domestic industry against more advanced international competitors.

Cosmetic quality should not be confused with cosmetic measures to give the product an attractive appearance, such as good looking packaging. This kind of cosmetics belongs to service quality, as it satisfies a real user's need.

Quality realized in the product or service will never cover exactly what is relevant and/or specified. Realized quality which is neither relevant nor specified is labeled *wasted quality*, as it serves no true purpose. Wasted quality is nihil in the engineer's ideal of Caesar's war chariot which never fails but at the end of its lifetime disappears completely into dust. If one bolt would still remain, then that bolt would have been constructed too conservatively and that would have had adverse weight implications. Unnecessary weight impairs the effectiveness of the chariot, which Caesar would never have accepted. This completes our classification of the seven categories of quality (Figure 3.2).

The classification enables us to formulate some recommendations to both the supplier and the buyer or user (Tables 3.1, 3.2).

Example: *Rules for truck manufacture*

After complying with the strict rules in regard to the dimensions of number plates in a certain country, a foreign truck manufacturer was faced with a new procedure for measuring the width of their trucks. The result was that their trucks exceeded the allowed maximum by 5 centimeters. When that issue was resolved by political pressure, a new law related to noise emission was issued,

Table 3.1 Recommendations on quality for the supplier

Quality improvement should be focused on the following categories:	
Category	Problem (if too high)
Non-realized crucial quality	Short term; one can rightly be blamed for not complying with the specifications
Non-realized service quality	Long term; image will be established as not being a quality supplier
Wasted quality	Long term; results in unnecessarily high cost price; image will be established as being an expensive supplier
Excuse quality • Useless to try to comply with; a new stick to hit with can always be found. • Focus actions on the real reason of exclusion; in case of protectionism try to obtain a local face.	

Table 3.2 Recommendations on quality for the buyer (user)

• Be flexible with regard to cosmetic quality and pay more attention to service quality.

• Exchanging some cosmetic quality for a little more service quality is often to the advantage of both the buyer and the supplier; this can be effected formally, i.e. via extra specifications, or informally in the acceptance procedure.

with the effect that his trucks were no longer allowed to drive in that country during specific night hours; the local manufacturer's trucks were just within the norm. This process was finally terminated by political pressure, such as threatening to ban the competitor's trucks from the roads of the home country by using similar (excuse) quality rules.

Example: *Rules for marine propeller manufacture*

After inspection of a finished marine propeller for a fast container vessel it turned out that it was somewhat out of tolerance at the inner sections. This does not impair its 'fitness for use' to any extent, since the margins against cavitation are more than enough for those sections and the strength is also hardly affected. At the outer sections, however, where the dimensions were within the specified tolerances, a higher dimensional accuracy would favorably influence the likelihood of cavitation erosion.

The manufacturer offered to finish the propeller according to this higher standard at the outer sections, rather than to that required by the agreed specifications. In exchange, the manufacturer asked for acceptance of the existing dimensions of the inner sections.

> This was accepted by the customer. Through the exchange of some cosmetic quality (inner sections) for some service quality (outer sections), the end user obtained a better quality for its purpose and the manufacturer could avoid a costly rejection of the propeller.

3.2 Use of the quality classification in the construction industry

In this section, we describe how our concept of the seven categories of quality was applied in the Nanhai project.

Prerequisite for the implementation of any new concept: the product champion

For the construction industry, the principle that compliance to specifications should be subordinated to real quality, i.e. fitness for purpose, constitutes a new concept. New ideas do not sell themselves. They need a product champion, also called organizational guerrilla, to achieve acceptance. The product champion fights with all available means for the acceptance of the innovation and is prepared to risk his reputation or even his job for it. A product champion is a prerequisite for the implementation of anything new in order to overcome the fear of innovation, which prevails in every organization. Machiavelli (15th century, in The Prince):

> There is nothing more difficult to take in hand, or more perilous to conduct, or more uncertain in its success, than to take the lead in the introduction of a new order of things because the innovator has for enemies all those who have done well under the old conditions, and only lukewarm defenders in those who may do well under the new.

Fortunately, our quality concept found its product champion in the person of Ton Sluman, who understood it and applied it in his daily work. He attached the pictures of the circles with associated one-liners on the publication board on the site (Figures 3.3, 3.4, 3.5, 3.6, 3.7).

Support for the product champion's approach was provided not only by the project team but also by the CEO of the entire project (Simon Lam). The prerequisite for acceptance of *a new order of things*, a product champion with the blessing of a benefactor high up in the organization, being satisfied in this case has been a key factor for its success.

The use of the quality circles

The Venn diagrams of our quality classification, usually referred to as *quality circles*, were used for three different purposes:

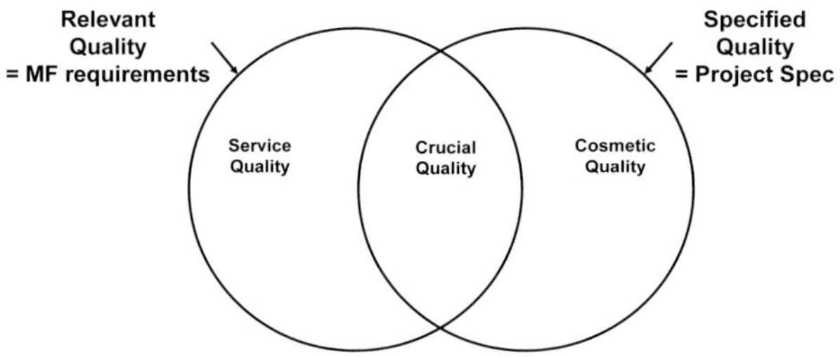

Figure 3.3 Specs never cover relevant quality.

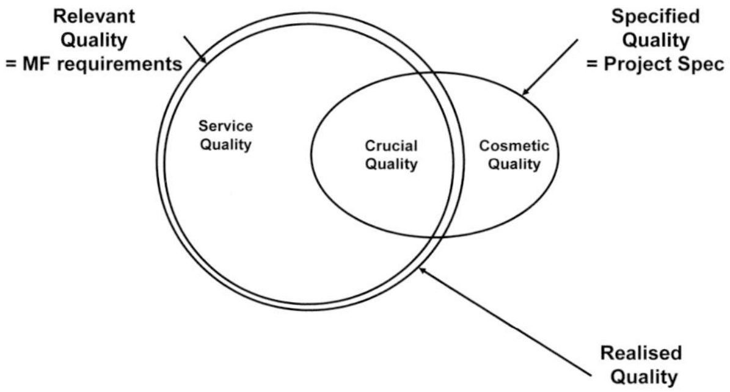

Figure 3.4 The ideal world.

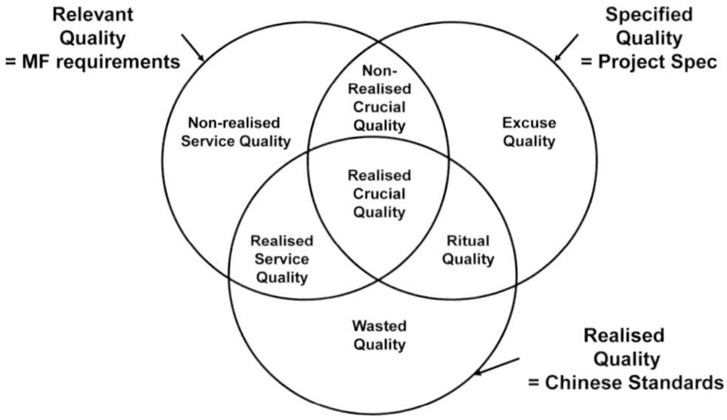

Figure 3.5 You do not get what you want or specified.

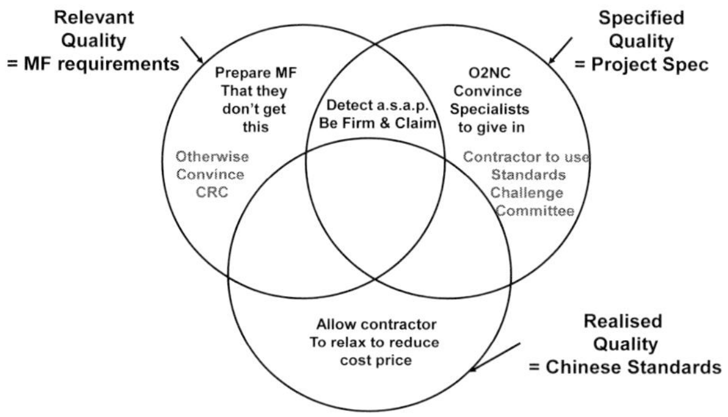

Figure 3.6 Communication is key.

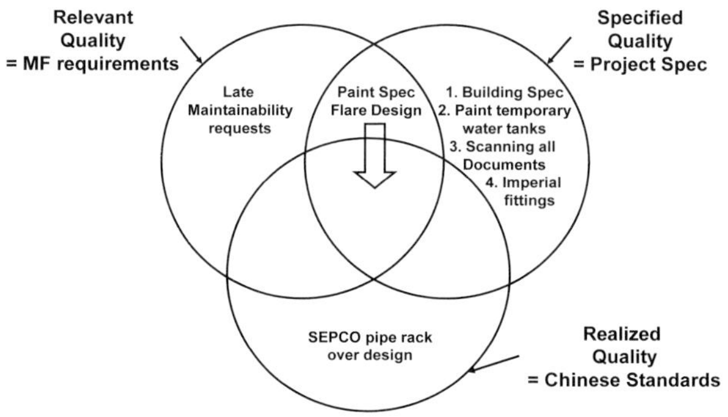

Figure 3.7 Examples.

1. *Accepting Chinese standards* whenever possible. For instance, accepting them for buildings not essential to the process of the plant, and relaxing the offshore Shell standards to Chinese ones for the jetty in the middle of Daya Bay.

2. *Changing scope.* Many small changes done in process to increase reliability and reduce costs. For instance, delaying the railway, since it could not yet be used by the future refinery next door and outsourcing the air splitter to Praxair adjacent to the site, who could make also nitrogen and oxygen for others, thereby utilizing economies of scale to the benefit of both parties.

3. *Managing expectations of maintenance departments* by providing them with records of non-conformance from original specifications for later use in inspection programs and debottlenecking studies.

Quality-related issues arose in all seven categories of quality, as is illustrated in the following examples:

1. *Non-realized service quality* (relevant, not specified, not realized). Hidden deficiencies which surface in the first commissioning phase and first years of operation.

2. *Non-realized crucial quality* (relevant, specified, not realized). Serious issues arose with the quality of underground water cooling lines due to sub-standard design by Chinese vendors, irregularities with licenses, and construction not according to specifications but to Chinese practices of drains. Awarding contract after competitive tendering to four different contractors entailed losing central control. Ultimately, a fall-back system (based on steel instead of glass fiber reinforced Epoxy) was installed, but so far has not been used.

3. *Realized service quality* (relevant, not specified, realized). Example 1: Because of accidents elsewhere, spheres for ethylene and propylene storage were under scrutiny. German materials were used which were better than prescribed by the Chinese authority for this matter. Nevertheless, a lobbying battle turned out to be needed for their approval. Example 2: Dredging by Chinese contractors without dumping. Monitoring for suspended soils and other environmental impact done by Boskalis was better than specified. Even a living choral was relocated. But Chinese authorities did not believe there had not been any dumping, invoked the license and wanted penalty fees to be paid. Instead of giving in to this, a budget was approved for additional inspection at a dumping station, twenty miles out of the coast in accordance with the London dumping convention. Apparently, it is so unusual to do better

than specified in regulations that this evoked problems instead of appreciation.

4. *Wasted quality* (not relevant, not specified, realized). Overdesign in engineering is quite common in China. The government holds engineering, which is kept completely separated from construction, responsible for eventual disasters. Chief Engineers of Chinese design institutes, trying to reduce the risk of sanctions (including prison sentence), tend to be conservative rather than cost-conscious. Construction, by contrast, is in China always trying to cut costs by compromising quality. For this reason, the government established specialized supervision companies to check on 'construction to design'. In the Nanhai project, the steel constructions for the power plant were overdesigned by Sepco, a Chinese power and construction company.

5. *Ritual quality* (not relevant, specified, realized). A big investment was made in the water treatment and solid waste disposal facilities. A twenty kilometer pipeline was laid under water to discharge at a point of maximum turbulence and mixing with tidal movements. Other local parties in similar situations refrained from such expensive measures, indicating that this was a case of ritual quality.

6. *Realized crucial quality* (relevant, specified, realized). Many issues surfaced in this category. One example is small bore connections: Chinese contractors were not sufficiently aware of the specifications and did not comply. Corrections were made on time with special inspection tools. A second example is flare construction, which was a copy of the plant in Pernis which can be lowered during operation. This requires sliding tolerances in millimeters. The Chinese vendor, not being sufficiently warned on this point, produced power tower quality with tolerances in centimeters. It was redone at the site, on time but at extra cost.

7. *Excuse quality* (not relevant, specified, not realized). Example 1: British scaffolding was specified, but Chinese standards were actually good enough. Halfway, Chinese standards were adopted with full enforcement of implementation. The benefits in regard to cost and time created goodwill with the contractors. Example 2: The project team considered the Shell safety systems to be overdone and took the liberty to not fully implement them, which proved to be justified in the start up. Example 3: Temporary water tanks were specified to be painted, which requirement was waived by the project team. Example 4: Buildings were specified with Shell standards. Two contractors for twelve buildings were allowed to build according to Chinese standards (with the exception of the

blast proof control rooms). Example 5: Some of the as-built documentation specifications were considered to be overdone and were waived.

For the authorization of the quality related changes, two committees were in function:

1. Change committee on scope changes, chaired by the CEO (Simon Lam).
2. Standard challenge committee, chaired by the construction director (Frans), which always involved the end user in its decision making.

Giving away cosmetic quality and wasted quality, or exchanging these for service quality, yields substantial cost savings for the contractors concerned and generates valuable goodwill with them. It is essential however that the changes are authorized at the right organizational level.

3.3 Trade-offs between quality, costs, and schedule

In construction projects, trade-offs must always be made between quality, costs and schedule. Quality is usually perceived as being defined by the project's specifications. Costs are supposed to be specified by the budget. The schedule is assumed to be given by a network planning aimed at completion on time. As a result, prevailing management focus in construction projects tends to be concentrated on cost and schedule, with quality management limited to implementing contractual specifications.

When construction projects become large and complex, however, many relevant matters are reflected neither in the contractual specifications nor in the budget or the network planning of the project. As a result, functionality suffers under the prevailing management approach. A costly effort must still be made to ensure that unspecified, yet relevant, quality is realised in the project. Inevitably, this leads to substantial overruns in time and money.

Attempts to avoid these overruns in time and money have resulted in ever more exhaustive specifications, budgets and schedules, but these turn out to produce disappointingly little effect. This is not surprising in view of the fact that the every-day reality is too complex to be realistically reflected in specifications, budgets and schedules. Even if that would be at all possible, it is naive to expect that subcontractors will take the time to fully read and digest such voluminous documentation, particularly within the limited time of the bidding phase.

In short, the usual preoccupation with cost and schedule does not work. As with the arts of Zen – archery, sword fighting, flower arranging – one has to remove the ultimate goal – the arrow hitting the target, striking the opponent, achieving the most beautiful flower arrangement – completely from the mind and concentrate on quality as required by functionality and not only as specified in contracts and consider cost and time of completion as outcomes of a process, which can only indirectly be controlled.

3.4 Charter and project team

The charter of a project consists of:

1. The *objectives* describing the functionality and quality to be achieved;
2. The *budget* specifying the agreed financial limits;
3. Target *time of completion* determining the agreed deadline for commissioning.

The charter is to be carried out by the project team.

When the project is large and complex, the project manager should not only have a stakeholder-oriented attitude himself, but the whole project team that supports him should display that attitude. Team members should be more than just capable in their profession. If they have a control-oriented, basically a PI, style of management, they are not suited for a project team from which a lot of PII-management is required.

When selecting members of the project team, therefore, an additional requirement to the usual selection criteria should be that they understand PII best management practices or the project leader will be isolated in his approach and become a prophet in the desert. In the Nanhai project, this requirement was clearly fulfilled in regard to the CEO, the construction director, and all other members of the project team, who therefore deserve collective credit for its success.

4 Scheduling with allowance for mitigations-on-the-run

Already in the early seventies I became aware of the usefulness of probabilistic network planning, nowadays referred to as PERT (Program Evaluation and Review Technique), for the scheduling of activities of a project. As a manufacturer of controllable pitch propellers we were confronted with a serious capacity problem: sales had doubled the turnover, but the required expansion of production capacity had been delayed by obstruction from our financial director who had his doubts about sales increasing the turnover as planned. The orders for new milling and drilling machines were many months delayed.

What we did to prevent the imminent claims from customers and serious damage to our reputation was the following:

1. We bought a PERT scheduling program, which was in use for the factories of Philips N.V., Eindhoven.

2. The input not only comprised our own production capacity but also that of our sub-suppliers.

3. We kept ourselves informed on delays that our customers, mainly shipyards, would incur anyway. If they were substantial, we knew that we could exceed contractual delivery times without any consequences.

4. The program was run at a weekly frequency. The output provided us with the best scheduling of activities: which production facility, both internal and external, to use for which customer's order.

In this way we survived the production capacity crisis without any claims or damage to our reputation.

In view of this positive experience, I was surprised to learn that Frans did not use (probabilistic) network planning for his day-to-day decision-making. He only used it 'to keep his board satisfied', as he put it, by answering their inevitable questions about 'The Critical Path'. Actually, there is no such thing as a Critical Path, as will become apparent from this chapter.

Our discussions on the subject finally enabled me to pinpoint the fundamental error in all current planning models: *The implicit assumption that execution will take place as indicated by the planning software*. In other words, that the project manager will sit down with his arms crossed and do nothing when things do not evolve as planned. In practice, however, he works his head off to correct things that do not proceed as planned. He takes all kind of measures – mitigations – to ensure that the target completion date of the project is achieved in spite of numerous things that do not develop according to plan. In short, planning software that does not account for mitigations on the run may be useful for control, but is unsuited for the (weekly) scheduling of activities.

To correct this fundamental error, I developed a probabilistic network methodology enabling mitigations on the run to be taken into account. Frans, however, was still not satisfied because the program could not allow for non-availability of qualified persons needed for envisaged mitigations. This led to incorporating an allowance for limited human resources.

The methodology, as published in de Graaf and van Gunsteren (2009), will be reproduced below. For a description of the state-of-the-art of probabilistic network planning without allowance for mitigations on the run, but including our new concept of risk ranking, we refer to Appendix A.

4.1 Different kind of mitigations

The prevailing practice of awarding contracts to the lowest bidders regardless of their quality track record and allowing relatively unknown local firms to bid inevitably results in at least some of them failing to deliver the quality required for full functionality of the entire project. When such failure to deliver relevant quality becomes apparent, what can the project manager do?

Heerkens (2001) lists the following options: 1) Push for compliance, 2) Recover in later tasks, 3) Add resources, 4) Use alternative work methods, 5) Offer incentives, 6) Renegotiate cost and schedule targets, 7) Reduce scope.

These options all constitute mitigations on the run, corrective measures to cope with the non-compliance of certain subcontractors. In addition, mitigations on the run are usually also required to address problems due to unforeseen events and developments during the construction period, such as a strike, a typhoon, or a delay in obtaining permits.

Two conditions have to be fulfilled for successful implementation of the mitigations:

1. A redundancy of capable people and financial resources has to be available to be assigned to the mitigations.
2. Forthcoming disasters have to be spotted at such an early stage that sufficient time is available for implementation.

These conditions can be incorporated in the probabilistic network planning of a project.

4.2 Probabilistic network planning state-of-the-art

Probabilistic network planning with PERT (Program Evaluation Review Technique) can be regarded as the current state-of-the-art in project network planning but it does not enable the modeling of mitigations on the run. See, for instance, Meredith and Mantel (2006). In deterministic network planning with CPM (Critical Path Method), single input values are given for the activity durations. In PERT, three estimates for an activity have to be provided: a pessimistic (p), a most likely (m), and a most optimistic estimate (o), which enables answers to be given to questions regarding the probability of finishing the project within a given time.

Critical Chain Planning (Leach, 2000) is a probabilistic network planning method aimed at an optimal allocation of a limited total of resources to be assigned to activities along the Critical Chain.

The probabilistic approach used in both PERT and Critical Chain Planning constitutes an improvement compared to the deterministic CPM approach, but it brings along a fundamental shortcoming: it only provides information on activities on one critical path. It may very well be that the critical path for achieving, say, a 90% probability of completion on time is different from the critical path calculated with the medians (best guesses) of the activity durations. This shortcoming is removed with the Monte Carlo based risk ranking as proposed by Binnekamp et al. (2006) and summarised in the next section.

In Render et al. (2003), a technique is offered to shorten, in the cheapest way, the duration of a project by reducing activity durations. The technique, called project crashing, is applicable only to the deterministic CPM planning method for which it seeks to speed up the project in the cheapest manner. In practice, however, the project manager should be primarily interested in speeding up the project in such a way that the probability of timely completion remains at an acceptable level at all times, and not in the cheapest way to do so with, possibly, a low probability of success.

4.3 Monte Carlo based risk ranking

As with PERT, for all activities the project is composed of, three estimates are made for the activity concerned: a most pessimistic, a most likely (best guess), and a most optimistic estimate. The pessimistic and optimistic estimates are defined as having a 10% probability of being exceeded. A skewed probability distribution, such as the beta distribution (see for instance Vose (2000)), is assumed through the three given estimates.

The Monte Carlo simulation is then conducted by carrying out a critical path calculation, say 2,000 times, using activity durations that are obtained from the skewed distributions (by drawing a random number which is corrected for the skewed distribution). The frequency distribution of the 2,000 calculations provides the probability distribution for the duration of the entire project. Additionally, a counter keeps track of how many times (out of the 2,000) a given path through the network was the critical path. This provides a ranking of the paths by their associated risk, that is, the likelihood that a given path will be the critical path in reality.

The risk ranking of the paths with their associated risks is important to the project manager, as it indicates how much attention should be paid to monitoring activities on the various paths. Additionally, the probability distribution for the completion of the entire project is, of course, of great interest to the financial stakeholder.

4.4 Allowance for mitigations in probabilistic network planning

Testing the usefulness of the methodology of the preceding section for a 4.3 billion dollar construction project (actually the Nanhai project) and deliberations with its project manager revealed the following:

1. The probability of completion on time according to the Monte Carlo simulation of the entire project is extremely low, in the order of a few percent.
2. This does not reflect reality, because the implicit assumption that no corrective measures (mitigations) are carried out is not realistic. In practice numerous measures are taken during execution, sometimes at considerable cost, to remove blocks to progress. In particular, trustworthy project managers (from the main contractor, subcontractors, or other sources) have to be mobilized. These are limited in number.

The latter consideration explains why in practice construction managers tend to be reluctant to use probabilistic network planning and prefer to stick to the familiar Gantt diagram for their day-to-day decision making. Winch (2002, pp. 265-267) gives three explanations for this reluctance: 1) The program becomes decoupled from the realities of the weekly management of the site, 2) It is used as a baseline against which progress is measured and payments are made, 3) The estimates for the activity durations are made by the people responsible for their implementation.

To avoid these disadvantages, planning tools should be focused on the needs of weekly management and be used, pro-actively, for operational decisions rather than for measuring progress. Unfortunately, in the current state-of-the-art of probabilistic network planning, the most important information for day-to-day decision making – the impact of possible mitigations – is missing.

The following mathematical model is proposed in order to incorporate such mitigations on the run in the network planning.

Optimization of mitigations

For each of the n activities A_i $(i = 1, 2, \ldots, n)$ three estimates for the duration t_i are made, including delays that have so far surfaced during execution:

1. Pessimistic estimate (probability of 0.1 that reality will be worse);

2. Best guess;

3. Optimistic estimate (probability of 0.1 that reality will be better).

Let us assume that m measures can be taken. Each measure results in reducing an activity A_i's time t_i by Δt_i at cost $C_i, i = 1, 2, \ldots, m$. In each Monte Carlo run, the following Linear Programming (LP) optimization is performed:

$$\text{Minimize} \quad \sum_{i=1}^{m} C_i \tag{4.1}$$

Subject to:

$$t_e \leq t_0 \tag{4.2}$$

Where t_e is the throughput time and t_0 is the target completion time.

In other words: minimize the use of mitigations, while staying within the target completion time. A counter keeps track of how often in the Monte Carlo simulation an activity duration is reduced by corrective measures. We then assume that, say, the most frequent four are indeed carried out. With these reduced activity durations, a new Monte Carlo simulation is conducted. If the probability of completion on time turns out to increase to, say, over 50%, the measures can be considered to be sufficient.

This procedure can be repeated at any stage of the project to assess what mitigations are desirable at that point in time. In this way, the probability of timely completion can be kept at an acceptable level during the whole execution of the project. Should this become infeasible, the necessity of relaxing the completion time becomes known at an early stage.

The project manager of before mentioned 4.3 billion dollar construction project regarded the incorporation of mitigations on the run in the scheduling software to be a major improvement of its usefulness in practice, but wished that non-availability of required key persons could also be taken into account. How that can be done is described below.

Allowing for limited human resources

Each mitigation C_i, Δt_i will require human resources R, each having one or more skills S. Given this information (Table 4.1), the Monte Carlo simulation of the preceding section can provide not only the set of mitigations C_i, Δt_i required to meet the deadline t_0 at an acceptable probability p, but also the

Table 4.1 Mitigations C_i, Δt_i, human resources R, and required skills S.

Skills	S_1	S_2	S_3	S_4
		Mitigations (demand)		
C_1, Δt_1	•			
C_2, Δt_2		•	•	
C_3, Δt_3	•	•		•
		Resources (supply)		
R_1		•		
R_2			•	
R_3	•			•

associated set of skills S required for implementing these mitigations. Subsequently, the minimum required project team can be obtained from the LP optimization:

$$\text{Minimize} \quad \sum_{k=1}^{K} R_k \tag{4.3}$$

Subject to:

$$a \leq a_0 \tag{4.4}$$

Where a represents the number of allocations per person and a_0 the maximum allocations per person.

This means that we minimize the size of the project team with the constraint that one person can be assigned to at most a_0 mitigations. This maximum a_0 should never exceed four because it has been established that even a very competent person cannot handle more than four tasks simultaneously.

The rationale for choosing the objective function (4.3) is that the smaller the project team is, the better it is. Each project team member brings along costs – and opportunity costs – related to mobilization and demobilization and time to become familiar with the project. Multi-skill persons, therefore, should be preferred above single-skill specialists.

The output of this second LP run, with objective function (4.3), provides the composition of the project team needed to carry out the mitigations (output of the first LP run, with objective function (4.1)).

Let us assume that one or more persons R of this project team cannot be made available. The first step then is to remove those C_i, Δt_i mitigations which require skills S that are no longer available. The Monte Carlo simulation is repeated with these corrected inputs, which reflects the situation of reduced human resources. When too many people are removed from Table 4.1, no

Table 4.2 Path ranking on risk and on slack.

Ranking	1st	2nd	3rd	4th	5th	6th
On risk	G	C	H	B	I	J
Percentage	22.35%	15.81%	12.16%	9.71%	9.28%	7.88%
On slack	A	B	C	D	E	F

solution will be found. This indicates that either the deadline t_0 for completion has to be relaxed, or more human resources have to be provided.

4.5 Application in a multi-billion dollar construction project

The methodology is illustrated with its application in the 4.3 billion dollar construction project. The associated software is referred to as MSP (Mitigations Scheduling Program).

Risk ranking

The (condensed) network consists of about 190 activities. Most of the activities have a Finish to Start relation. Some have a Finish to Finish relation. In addition to the expected duration (best guess), estimates on pessimistic and optimistic durations are added to each activity. These estimates are based on the experience of the project managers involved. With this information, a Monte Carlo simulation is carried out. This results in the path ranking shown in Table 4.2. For comparison, the path ranking based on slack in deterministic CPM planning is also given.

Path A, identified as The Critical Path based on the deterministic approach, is not the path that was most critical based on the probabilistic approach. Even more surprising: According to the Monte Carlo simulations, Path A was never critical.

Path G, ranked as the most critical in the risk ranking, does not have a high position when ranked based on slack. Should the project manager use the ranking on slack to identify which paths to pay particular attention to, path G would not get appropriate attention.

It turns out that six different paths (not including 'The Critical Path' A!) have substantial associated risk (frequency of being the critical path in the Monte Carlo simulation), indicating that they should get particular attention from the project management.

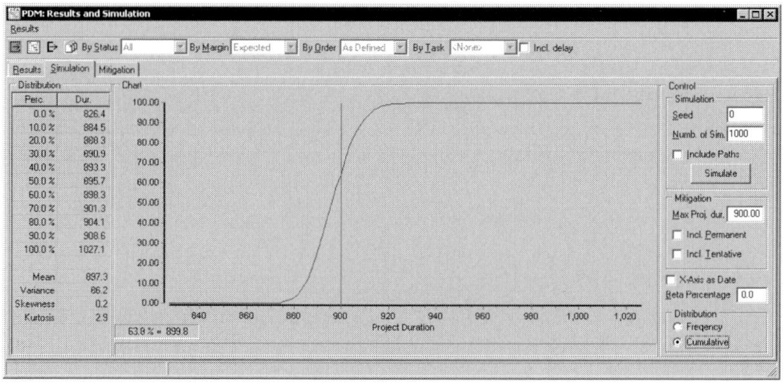

Figure 4.1 MSP results: no mitigations.

Simulation of mitigations on the run

The Monte Carlo simulation of the initial planning in Figure 4.1 shows a probability of completion within the target of 900 days of 64%. As the project progressed, five activities incurred delays as given in Table 4.3. This reduced the probability of completion on time to 47%, which was considered unacceptable. Nine possible mitigations with associated costs and time gains were identified (Table 4.3), and used in the Monte Carlo simulation (Figure 4.2).

Combinations of the three most effective mitigations, with the associated probability of completion within 900 days, are given in Table 4.4. It can be seen that implementing all three brings the probability of completion on time to 69%, which is above the original level.

Eight candidates (resources) having skills as given in Table 4.5 were available for implementation of mitigations. The skills required for the best four mitigations (as established by the Monte Carlo simulations) are also given in Table 4.5. Skill 5, required for both mitigations PBP015 and PBO015, is only available once. The least used of the two, mitigation PBO15, is therefore excluded from the list, and is replaced by the number four, PAM140. This brings the probability of completion within 900 days to 70%.

4.6 Progress control

Network planning is not intended to control progress but to schedule activities for a project, preferably at a weekly frequency. When the network planning software is abused for control purposes, the reliability of the input – in particular the estimates of activity durations – will suffer because the individuals making the estimates will apply a hidden safety margin in order to avoid personal trouble later on.

Table 4.3 Activity durations, original and delayed, and potential mitigations.

Mitigation	Original			Delayed			Δt	Costs
	Opt.	Est.	Pess.	Opt.	Est.	Pess.		
PAM060	65	75	95	69	79	110		
PAM140		63					7	250
PBO005	50	60	100	52	63	105	10	560
PBO015	90	95	125	95	100	132	10	300
PBO025	95	100	130	100	105	137	20	1000
PBP005		40					5	790
PBP015		35					5	100
PBP035	85	90	115	93	99	127	10	350
PBP065		60					10	420
PKO025		180					40	2000

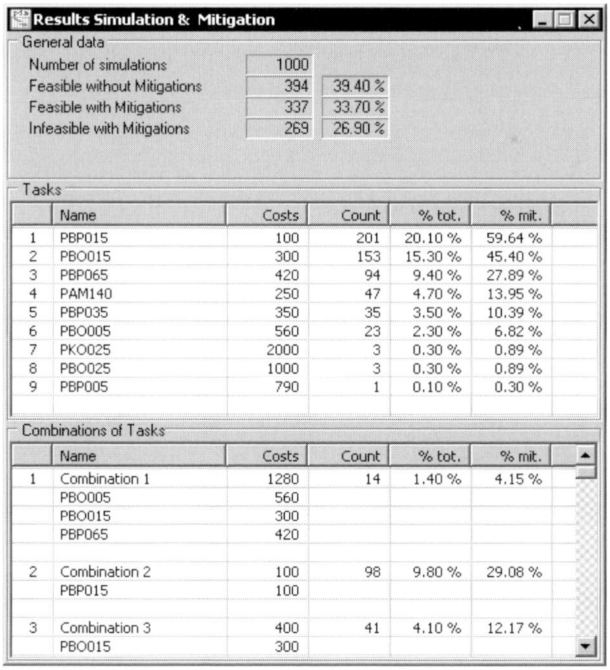

Figure 4.2 MSP results: various combinations of mitigations.

Table 4.4 Applied mitigations and probability of timely completion.

Mitigations	Probability of timely completion
No mitigations	47%
PBP015	59%
PBP015 & PBO015	63%
PBP015, PBO015, & PBP065	69%

Table 4.5 Resources, mitigations, and required skills.

Skills	1	2	3	4	5	6	7	8	9	10
Resources (supply)										
1	•			•				•		
2	•			•		•			•	
3		•		•					•	
4	•	•		•			•			
5			•		•		•			
6			•			•		•	•	
7		•		•			•			•
8								•		•
Mitigations (demand)										
PAM140	•			•		•			•	
PBO015			•		•			•		•
PBP015	•			•	•			•		
PBP065	•			•			•			

Progress control can be achieved by:

1. Milestones. Define measurable results and observe when they are achieved.

2. Resources, man-hours or dollars, actually spent versus planned or budgeted (Figure 4.3). This is of particular importance at early stages: a week at the beginning of a project is as important as a week at the end.

3. Make the intuition of the project leader explicit (Figure 4.4).

Man-hours plotted against time only say something about invested effort but nothing about results. To this end, the project leader should estimate, after preset amounts of expenditure, how much money is still needed to reach the project objectives or the next measurable milestone.

Say, after spending 10 percent of the budget, the project leader feels that 95 percent of the budget is still needed to finish the project, and not 90 percent as expected. If no further setbacks occur, the line will be continued under 45 degrees and the project leader will end up with a 5 percent budget overrun. The chart allows one to see at an early stage if a project is getting out of hand. Normally, projects show a few kinks at the beginning of the curve and a few at the end. The former are due to technical roadblocks that were not foreseen in the feasibility study, the latter represent the unpleasant surprises that seem unavoidable when anything has to be completed.

Various forms of the chart in Figure 4.4 exist in practice, but all are based on the same principle, namely making the intuition of the project leader explicit. In conventional financial accounting only the past is recorded and nothing is reported on the future. This is a major handicap for taking timely corrective measures. The concept of Figure 4.4 remedies this shortcoming.

Example: *Foreman's estimate of delivery time*

In addition to making the intuition of the project manager explicit, it can be useful to consult other persons who are directly involved. As managing director of a shipyard for off-shore equipment I was confronted with what I felt was a too ambitious planning for the delivery of a drill ship. The responsible deputy director maintained his view that his planning was realistic. One of our foremen, 64 years old, had started working with the yard when he was a boy of 14 years, so he had fifty years working experience (and was still very active). I asked him what his feeling was in regard to the delivery time of the vessel. Initially, he reminded me that he was not responsible for the planning, but those 'expensive engineers from the university'. I agreed with that, but also said that it surprised me that he had no opinion on the matter, despite his

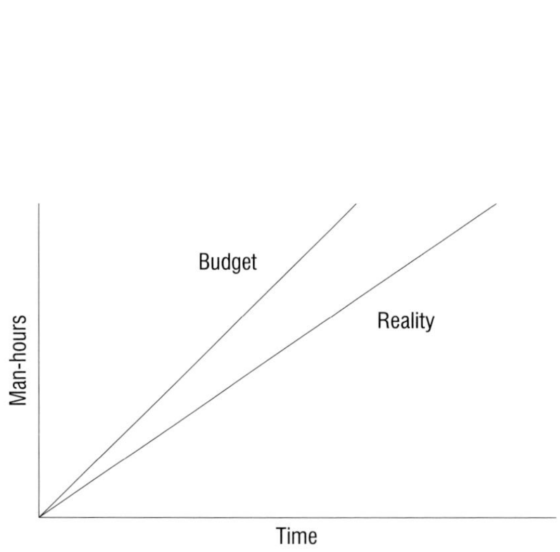

Figure 4.3 Project control: accumulated budget and realized man-hours versus time. A week at the beginning of a project is as important as a week at the end!

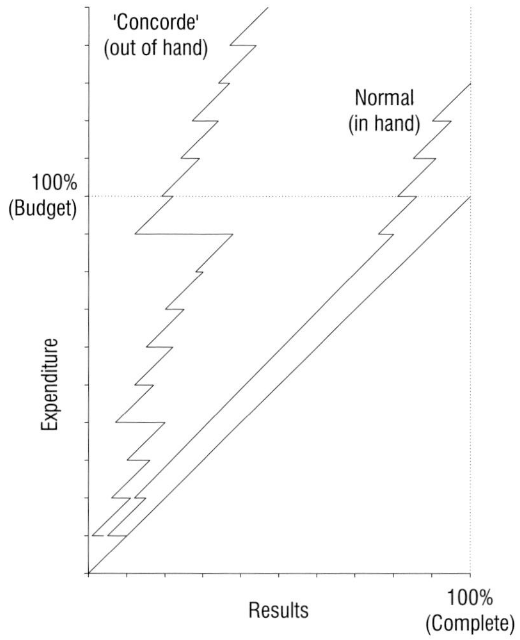

Figure 4.4 Project control: Make the intuition of the project leader explicit. At regular intervals the project leader should estimate how much money (and time) is still needed!

fifty years of experience. He then felt challenged, took some moments to think and gave me his estimate, which was about seven weeks later than the official planning. I decided to keep the later date as a basis for our dealings with the customer and other parties involved. The estimate of our experienced foreman turned out to be exactly right. Our deputy director is still puzzled how I could know that his planning was too optimistic.

5 Selection of subcontractors

An unfortunate choice of subcontractors can have disastrous consequences for the project as a whole.

> **Example:** *Carriages for the Amsterdam-Paris High Speed Train*
>
> An Italian manufacturer, being the lowest bidder, was awarded the contract in spite of their bad reputation in regard to living up to commitments. When they did not keep the agreed delivery times the whole project incurred delays in the order of years rather than months.

This example illustrates that reputation matters. One of the first lessons taught to me when I joined the Royal Boskalis Westminster Group in the late seventies, at that time (and today) the world's market leader in dredging contracting, was: 'Once we have started the construction of a harbor, we will finish it, no matter what.' Disputes about payments should never interfere with the progress of the project concerned. They should be settled by separate negotiation or arbitration. This company policy reveals the stakeholder-oriented attitude of the dominant coalition of the Boskalis Group, which in due course established its reputation of reliability.

Most people realize that awarding contracts exclusively on price can be penny-wise and pound-foolish. Nevertheless, the bidding price tends to dominate almost always the decision-making process.

For example, a project team had agreed that they would ignore any price difference smaller than 5% and that in such cases other criteria than price would be decisive. But when that turned out to be not so easy, one member of the team proposed to award the contract to the lowest bidder whose bid was 2% lower than that of the second best. Apparently, there is a need to facilitate multi-criteria decision-making.

In this chapter, a software tool* is offered for this purpose, based on the theory of Preference Function Modeling (Barzilai, 2010).

5.1 Tetra software for multi-criteria decision-making

The purpose of this section is to give the reader an overview of the steps involved in using the Tetra decision making software to evaluate choices using preference function modeling. Tetra comes in two versions: One of which is used by a single decision maker (SDM). It is 'standalone,' in that everything

*See http://www.scientificmetrics.com/ for more information and an evaluation version.

is installed on a single computer, and all model information is stored in documents on that computer. The other is for group decision making (GDM). It is based on the use of a Tetra server, and all model information is stored on the server, allowing it to be accessed by users running Tetra on multiple workstations on a network. As the use of both versions is identical in many respects, this description covers both versions, pointing out the differences where appropriate.

You will see how to use Tetra to evaluate a number of alternatives, based on criteria organized in a hierarchical manner. The alternatives are rated on each of the criteria. In the case of SDM a single evaluator specifies his or her ratings. With GDM multiple decision makers can participate in the process.

The process of using Tetra to make a decision consists of eight steps:

1. Create a model.
2. Define the Decision Makers who will be involved in the process (GDM only).
3. Define the alternatives to be considered in making the decision.
4. Define the criteria upon which the decision will be based. These criteria may be defined in a tree-like structure, using main criteria, sub-criteria, sub-sub-criteria, and so on.
5. Define the weights for all the criteria. These are defined relatively, specifying how important each criterion is in relation to others. The weights are defined in each node of the criteria tree.
6. Establish reference alternatives for each criterion.
7. Each Decision Maker enters his or her ratings for each alternative with respect to each criterion.
8. 'Solve' the model that has been created by the previous steps to compute the overall scores and get a numerical rating of the alternatives that corresponds to the combined ratings of all of the Decision Makers.

5.2 Example: Buying a house

Step 1 – Creating and Opening a Model

In Tetra SDM, simply select New... under the File menu, or click on the New Model icon in the tool bar. You will be prompted to select a location to save the model file. Once you have done this, move on to Step 3.

In Tetra GDM, models are created on a server, and each client is set up for access to the server using the Tetra GDM Administration Tool. Information on creating models is contained in the online help for the Tetra GDM Administration Tool. Once a model has been created, and your computer is set up to access the Tetra server, you will need the following information to access the model:

- The server on which the model is located
- The name of the model
- Your personal username and password for the model
- The model password used by everyone accessing the model

Choose Open Model... under the File menu, and provide the necessary information. In Tetra GDM there is the option of opening the model in Exclusive Mode. This can only be done by the Model Owner, and allows viewing of all the Decision Maker ratings.

Step 2 – Defining Decision Makers (Tetra GDM Only)

In Tetra GDM the Model Owner specifies other users who can access the model. To do this, open the model as described above, and then choose Edit Decision Makers... under the File menu.

There are three different types of access that can be provided to models:

- Model Owner: This user is created in the process of creating the model using the Tetra GDM Administration Tool. The Model Owner is the only user who can define and modify the model. Like Decision Makers, the Model Owner can also specify ratings. The Model Owner is also responsible for defining the other users who have access to the model.
- Decision Maker: These users can view a model and specify their ratings for the alternatives based on the criteria defined. They cannot see weights or the ratings of other Decision Makers.
- Read Only: This type of user can only view the alternatives and criteria of the model, and cannot make any changes, specify or view any weights, or specify ratings. If this user was a Decision Maker at some time in the past, and specified ratings then, these ratings would still be visible to the user, but they would not be editable.

There are two primary uses of Read Only users. The simplest is when you want to have a user who can view the alternatives and criteria, but who will not be providing ratings for the decision making process. In this case, be sure to set the weight of the user to zero. Another use for Read Only users is to ‘freeze’ the ratings of a Decision Maker. To do this, the Model Owner can

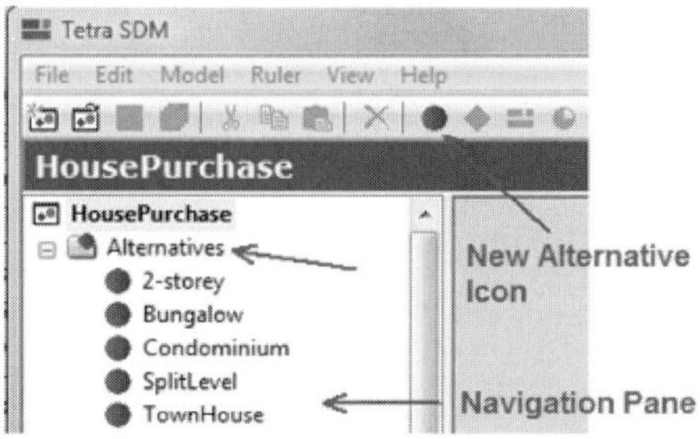

Figure 5.1 Creating alternatives.

choose Edit Decision Makers... under the File menu, select the desired Decision Maker, and then change the type of a Decision Maker user to Read Only. In this case you should leave the weight of the user as is, and not change it to zero, as doing so would remove that user's ratings from the computation of the model solution.

You should work through this procedure initially as the Model Owner, with no additional Decision Makers defined. Once you have completed this guide, create at least one Decision Maker, and one Read Only user, then close the model and reopen it as each of these users to explore the differences in access privileges. Once the model has been defined, if you are accessing the model as a Decision Maker skip to Step 7. If you are a Read Only user, you can simply browse the model, using the on-line help if necessary.

Step 3 – Identify Alternatives

Remember that, in Tetra GDM, you must be the Model Owner, and have the model opened in exclusive mode, in order to perform this step.

Suppose you have narrowed the choice to 5 acceptable homes: a bungalow, a split-level, a 2-storey house, a townhouse and a condominium.

Tetra actions to create alternatives (Figure 5.1):

- Right-click on the word Alternatives in the Navigation Pane and Select New Alternative (or click on the New Alternative icon in the toolbar) once for each of your five alternatives, and name the five houses accordingly.

Step 4 – Define Criteria

Remember that, in Tetra GDM, you must be the Model Owner, and have the model opened in exclusive mode, in order to perform this step.

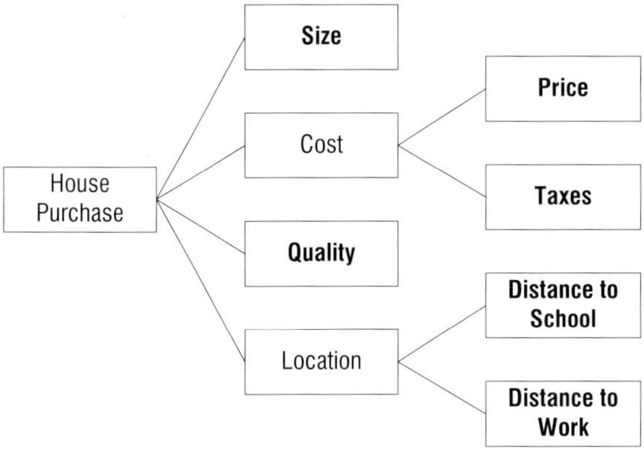

Figure 5.2 Defining criteria.

Assume that house Size, Cost, Quality and Location are your main criteria for making the decision. Furthermore, assume that your preference for the location actually depends on two sub-criteria: Distance to Work, and Distance to School for the children. Also, with respect to cost, you realize that you are concerned with the Taxes as well as the purchase Price (two more sub-criteria). The evaluation criteria are shown in Figure 5.2.

The method requires that you only state your ratings for the last level of sub-criteria on any branch, in this case the six bolded criteria.

Tetra actions to create criteria (Figure 5.3):

- Right click on the word Criteria in the criteria tree and select New Criterion (or click on the new criterion icon in the toolbar) once for each of your four main criteria, and name them accordingly.

Tetra actions to create sub-criteria:

- Select a criterion (such as Cost) in the criteria tree for which you want to enter sub-criteria, and now when you right click on it and select New Criterion (or click on the new criterion icon) new branches are created under the selected criterion. Observe that, when you define a sub-criteria, the icon of the criterion you create it below is changed from a simple criterion icon to a criteria folder icon.

- Repeat this process for all sub-criteria. Create price and taxes sub-criteria for the cost part of the hierarchy, and create distance to school and distance to work sub-criteria for the location part of the hierarchy.

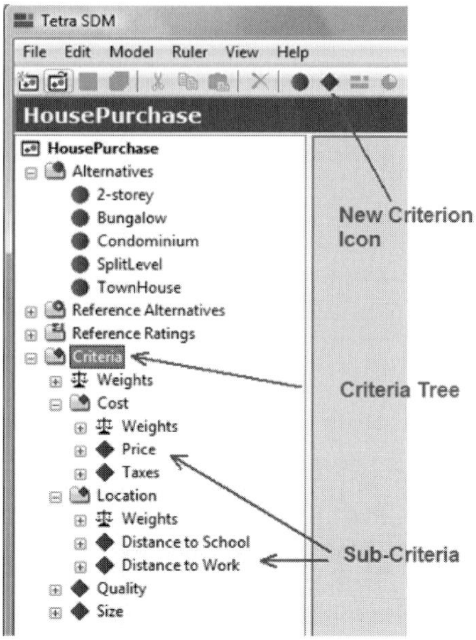

Figure 5.3 Creating criteria.

Step 5 – Assign Weights to the Criteria

Remember that, in Tetra GDM, you must be the Model Owner, and have the model opened in exclusive mode, in order to perform this step.

Defining the weights establishes the relative importance of the various criteria involved in making the decision. Weights are assigned using the same hierarchy as the criteria tree.

Tetra actions to create a set of weights (Figure 5.4):

- Right click on the word Weights in the model tree, immediately below the top-level criteria folder and Select New Weighting Ruler, or select the word Weights under the top-level criteria folder and click on the New Weighting Ruler icon in the toolbar. You may give the set of weights a name if you like.

- Double-click on the label for the current set of weights in the criteria tree ('Buyer 1' in this case). A blank weighting ruler will appear in the ruler area.

- Right click anywhere in the ruler area, select Add Criterion, then Add All. The resulting figure is shown below.

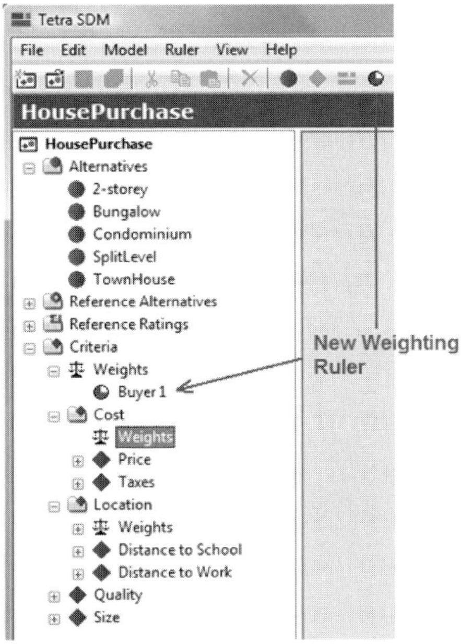

Figure 5.4 Creating weights.

- The weights are relative, so the method works by setting one criterion as a 'standard' against which the importance of another one is specified. Tetra initially sets one arbitrary criterion as the reference weight (Size in the figure), with a magnitude indicated by the red bar. The blue bar is associated with one other criterion weight (Quality in the figure). The length of the blue bar relative to the red bar, quantified by the boxed percentage between the rulers in the figure, corresponds to the relative importance of these two criteria (i.e. Quality is 80% as important as Size in the default set-up shown below).

Tetra actions to assign the weights for the top-level criteria (Figure 5.5):

- Right click the criterion label on the weighting ruler that you want to use as the standard (say Cost), and select Set Right. The red bar is now associated with the Cost criterion.

- Click on the Cost criterion on the ruler, and drag it somewhere to the right of all the other criteria. Then right click in a blank area of the ruler window, and select Expand. This changes the view of the ruler for easier visualization – it does not alter the values of any of the weights.

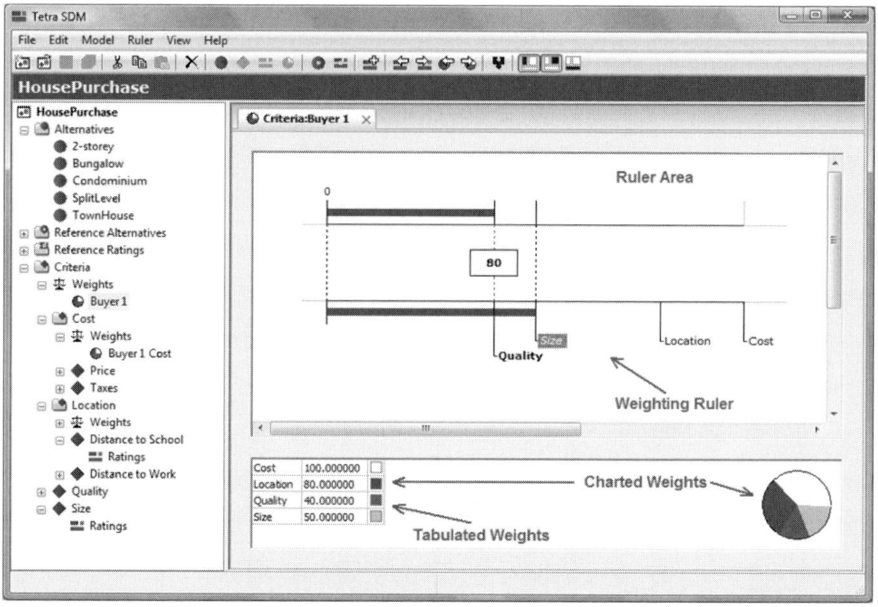

Figure 5.5 Assigning weights: size criterion.

- Drag the label for one criterion at a time in the figure, until its weight (or relative importance) relative to Cost is where you want it. For example, suppose that you consider the Location of the house to be 80% as important in your decision-making as the Cost factor; then drag the Location label until the proportion of the blue bar to the red bar is 80%, as shown in Figure 5.6.

- Repeat this procedure for the remaining two criteria, assuming for this exercise that house Size is 50% as important as the Cost, and that the Quality criterion is assigned a 40% weight relative to Cost.

- (Optional) You may enter more precise values directly into the Tabulated Weights cells in the lower pane. These proportions are reflected in the Ruler Window.

- Note that it is only the relative values of weights that are significant. For example, the same result would be obtained if two criteria, Size and Cost were given weights of 1 for Size and 2 for Cost or 50 for Size and 100 for Cost.

Tetra actions to assign the weights for the sub-criteria:

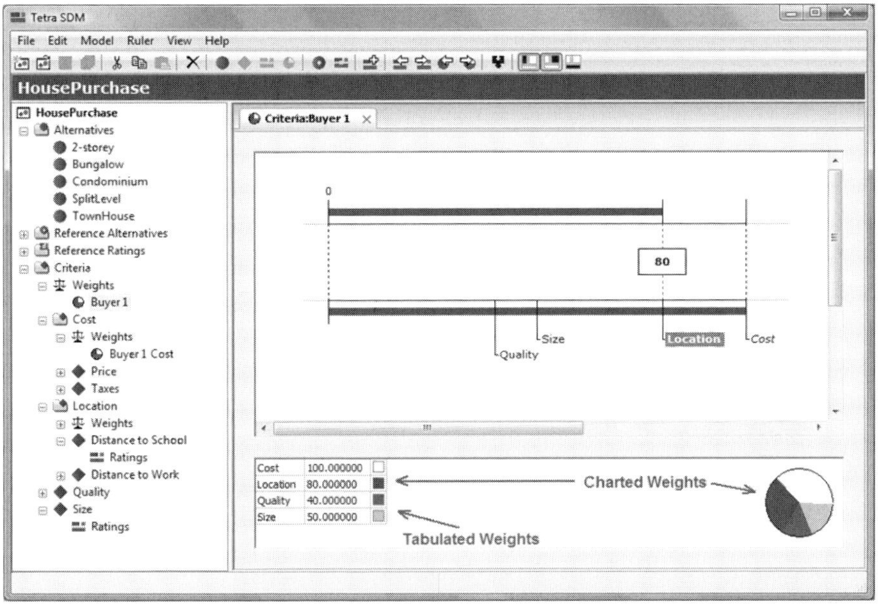

Figure 5.6 Assigning weights: location criterion.

This procedure is essentially the same as the preceding step, except for two variations:

- Start by clicking on the Weight label in the criteria tree that is associated with the sub-criteria for which you want to assign weights. As shown in the figure, to assign weights to the two sub-criteria associated with Cost, right click on the word Weight under the Cost branch, select New Weighting Ruler, and then continue as above.

- When right clicking on the weighting ruler to add criteria, only the set of corresponding sub-criteria will be available (Price and Taxes in this case).

- To complete the weighting of sub-criteria, set the sub-criterion Taxes to be 20% of the weight of Price, and the sub-criterion Distance To Work to have an importance weight of 40% relative to Distance To School.

A different perspective to entering weights is to think in terms of ratios. For example, if you consider Price to be 5 times as important as Taxes for making your decision, you could enter a value of 1.0 in the Taxes cell in the tabulated weights, and a value of 5.0 in the Price cell (Figure 5.7). The length of the red

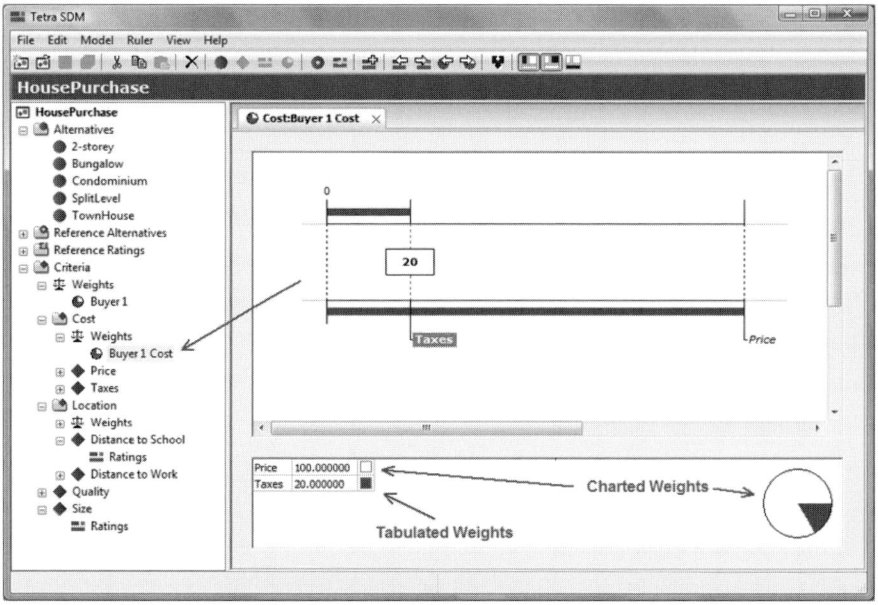

Figure 5.7 Assigning weights in terms of ratios.

and blue bars in the weighting ruler will adjust accordingly. (You can then expand the ruler to give the figure above).

As you work on weighting (and, later, on ratings), remember that changes you make to rulers are not automatically saved as you go along. You must either close the ruler (the X in the ruler tab), or save the changes with the Save Ruler or Save All Rulers commands in the Ruler menu.

Step 6 – Establish reference alternatives for each criterion.

At least two reference alternatives must be defined for each criterion on which the alternatives (the five houses) are rated, in order to establish a scale. This can be done by selecting a reference rating ruler or by associating actual or hypothetical objects with the default reference objects 'Z' and 'H' where 'Z' is an alternative or object that scores zero for that criterion and 'H' is an object that scores 100 for that criterion. Note that the reference alternatives are objects, i.e. their definition requires nouns rather than adjectives.

- Using hypothetical alternatives: For example, a hypothetical 'Z'-object for the Quality criterion could be a squalid bachelor apartment and a hypothetical 'H'-object for the Quality criterion could be a mansion.

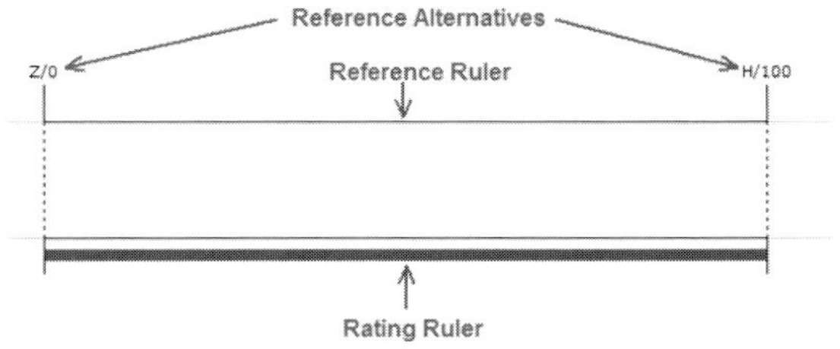

Figure 5.8 Reference alternatives.

Table 5.1 Extreme alternatives.

Criteria	Bottom	Top
Price	2-storey	Townhouse
Taxes	2-storey	Condominium
Distance to School	Bungalow	Split-level
Distance to Work	2-storey	Condominium
Quality	Townhouse	2-storey
Size	Condominium	2-storey

- Using actual alternatives: Another way to establish 'Z' and 'H' reference objects is to use two of the current alternatives. In our example, the 'Z'-object for the Quality criterion could be the townhouse, and the 2-storey house may serve as 'H'-object.

There are no Tetra actions required for this step - all that is needed is a clear definition of the reference alternatives for each of the six end-criteria, so that when ratings are made in the next step, they are done relative to these reference objects. Figure 5.8 shows how these concepts relate to the rating tools which will be invoked in the next section.

Suppose that the extreme alternatives associated with each of the six criteria are as stated in Table 5.1.

Note that for Price, the 'H'-object is the cheapest alternative and the 'Z'-object is the most expensive. For Distance to School, the 'H'-object was chosen as the closest alternative and the 'Z'-object is the farthest away.

In some decision-making situations, an Evaluation Plan is set up for the purpose of assessing future alternatives. In this case, the criteria are defined, weights selected, and reference alternatives are established in advance. Since the actual alternatives are not known when the Evaluation Plan is set up, hypothetical alternatives must be used to define the reference objects in the Evaluation Plan for each criterion.

Step 7 – Rating the alternatives against each criterion

All of the alternatives (the five houses) must be rated according to each of the six end-criteria.

If you are using Tetra GDM, this step is carried out by each of the Decision Makers involved. After you finish working through this guide as the Model Owner, create another Decision Maker, close the model and reopen it as this Decision Maker. Enter ratings for that Decision Maker using the same process described here, then close and open the model as the Model Owner again, so you can solve the model again to see the changes in the combined ratings.

When you open the model in Tetra GDM you have the option of opening it in 'Exclusive Mode.' This can only be done by the Model Owner, and allows the model owner to view (but not modify) the ratings of other Decision Makers. This is particularly useful when reviewing ratings as a group, as it makes it easy to move between and compare the ratings of all the Decision Makers involved in the process.

Tetra actions to rate alternatives against criteria:

- Right click on any criterion in the criteria tree (such as Quality) and select New Rating Ruler (or click on the new rating ruler icon in the menu bar) to create a new rating ruler. You may enter a name for this set of ratings if you choose (such as BuyerName).

- Double click the label for the current set of ratings ('BuyerName' in this case) in the criteria tree and a blank rating ruler will appear in the ruler area.

- Right click anywhere in the ruler area, select Add Alternative, then Add All.

- Using values from the table below, enter the ratings of the alternatives for each of the end-criteria. Note that for some criteria, such as Price, a higher value is worse; so in this example the more expensive 2-storey house is rated the lowest on the Price criterion.

Once you have the alternatives on the rating ruler, you can specify values for the ratings of each alternative in two ways:

- You can enter numerical values into the value entry table below the ruler.

- You can drag the alternatives along the ruler to specify the ratings.

In addition to specifying ratings for alternatives, Tetra also lets you specify relative ratings between alternatives. To do this, lower and upper alternatives are used. By default, the value 0 (reference alternative Z/0) is used for the

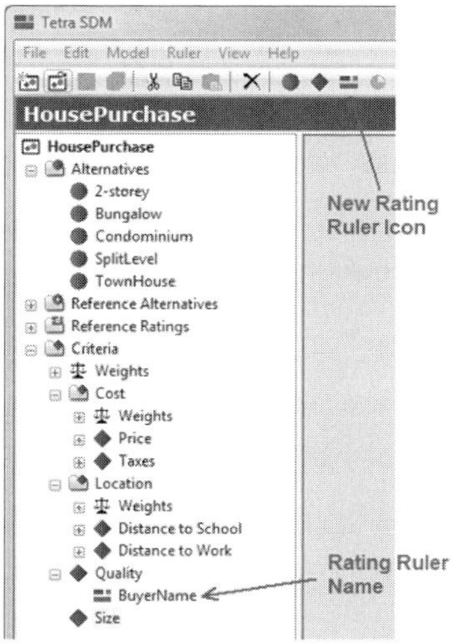

Figure 5.9 Creating rating rulers.

lower reference alternative, and the value 100 (reference alternative H/100) is used for the upper reference alternative. To choose a different lower or upper reference alternative, right click on the alternative or reference alternative you wish to use and choose Set Left or Set Right, respectively. In the figure, the Townhouse has been set to be the lower alternative and the 2-storey has been set to be the upper alternative.

In the rating ruler, the red bar indicates the difference between the upper and lower alternatives. When an alternative is selected, the blue bar indicates the difference between this alternative and the lower alternative and the green bar indicates the difference to the upper one. Furthermore, the value in the box on the line above the selected alternative shows the relative rating of the selected alternative as compared to the lower and upper alternatives (the ratio of the blue bar to the red one). In the figure we see that the Condominium is rated as being half-way between the Townhouse and the 2-storey with respect to this criterion. You can set the lower and upper alternatives back to the value 0 or the value 100 by right clicking anywhere in the rating ruler and choosing Clear Left or Clear Right, respectively.

Figure 5.10 shows what the rating ruler for one of the criteria, Distance to School, might look like.

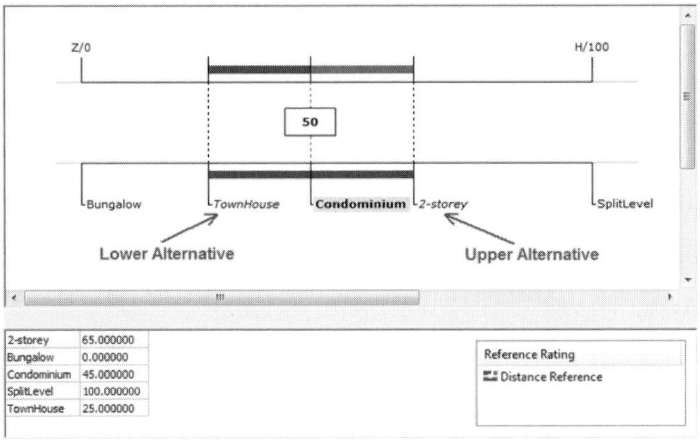

Figure 5.10 Rating alternatives.

Step 8 – Solve the Model to Determine the Preferred Alternative

Remember that, in Tetra GDM, you must be the Model Owner, and have the model opened in exclusive mode, in order to perform this step.

The preference function modeling methodology can now be applied to rank the five alternatives (the houses) according to their rating on each of the six criteria, and the relative importance of the criteria.

Tetra actions to run the solver (Figure 5.11):

- Click on the Solve icon in the menu bar.
- The results of the numerical ranking, the Overall Preference Scale, are shown in the solution output dialog.
- Using ratings and weightings similar to those presented in this example yields an overall preference scale such as the one in the screen capture. According to this result, the best decision is to buy the Split-Level house.

It should be noted that the Tetra software presupposes that the alternatives are known. That means it offers and evaluation method, not a design method in which the alternatives are not known *a priori*. Binnekamp (2010) has developed a methodology enabling a design to be based on the preferences of stakeholders, thereby making it possible to involve them already in the design stage of a project.

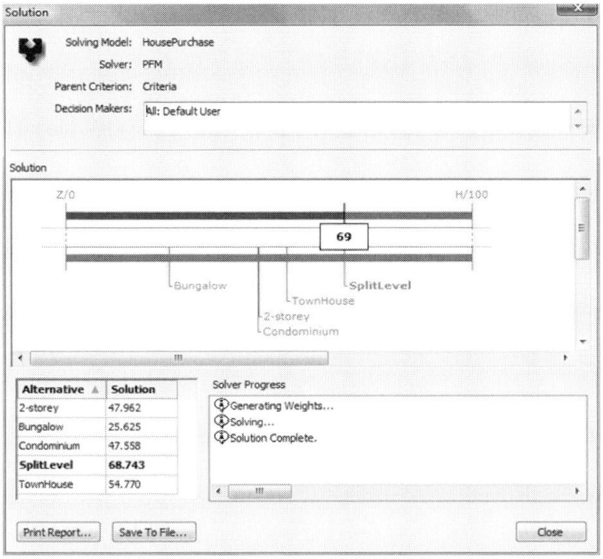

Figure 5.11 Solving the model.

5.3 An application of preference measurement in the construction industry

The importance of correct scaling of preferences is illustrated in the following application in the construction industry.

A reputable construction company used to address their customers with a yearly survey to measure their perception of the quality of the firm. Respondents were requested to give a grade, on a scale of 1 to 10, for the performance of the company in regard to various criteria that were considered to be relevant:

- Communication;
- Reliability;
- Delivery times;
- Eye for customer's interests;
- Quality control;
- Image.

On all criteria the company scored well above seven, so everything seemed to be in order. Until, that is, one of our graduates (Sneekes, 2003) raised the question: 'How do you know that your major competitors don't score an eight?'

After all, to be selected in a bidding procedure, to be 'good' is not good enough. One has to be perceived as better than the competing candidates. The answer was: 'We don't know, but we cannot ask our customers how we score compared to specific competitors.' This problem was resolved by asking each respondent to provide three scores per criterion:

- Score of the firm;
- Score of the worst competitor the respondent had ever experienced;
- Score of the best competitor ever experienced.

There was no need to disclose the identities of those worst and best performing competitors. This simple change in the survey made it possible to establish how the company scored in comparison to the competition. The company's objective was to score at least in the top quartile in all criteria. With the assumption that performance of competitors follows a normal distribution, the relative position of the firm on each criterion could be assessed. It turned out that on two criteria the firm scored just below the top quartiles, suggesting a need for managerial measures in those areas.

This example from practice shows how easily one can fool oneself if the measurement scales of preferences are not properly defined. The earlier survey results were completely meaningless, if not misleading. As becomes apparent, there exists no independent scale on which preference can be measured. There is no (known) zero-point (origin) representing the lowest preference. One cannot say: 'I like my new car twice as much as my old one.' To measure preference correctly, measurements have to be taken relative to two arbitrarily chosen reference points. What is measured is the ratio of differences and this operation is independent of the chosen origin and selected unit of measurement.

6 Information handling

Stakeholder-oriented management can only be effective when you know who the stakeholders are, what their interests are, and how their importance changes in different stages of the project. As this information is not readily available, the project manager has to find his own ways to get hold of this relevant information. On the other hand, the project manager tends to be flooded with a stream of, actually less relevant, information contained in standard reports on costs, progress, claims, etc.

In this chapter, an approach is offered to coping with the ever-increasing overabundance of information which tends to paralyze the manager of any large, complex project (Van Gunsteren, 1988).

6.1 A typology of information

Let us consider the case of a manager who has to make a decision. If God himself were to make that decision, He could make use of all the information relevant to the matter concerned. This information is labeled *relevant information* (Figure 6.1).

The manager, of course, receives much more information than he is ever able to use for his particular decision. This information is labeled *information paid attention to.* The part of that information that has relevance to the purpose concerned - the decision to be taken - is called *used information.*

Relevant information to which no attention is paid, is labeled *Cassandra information.* The god Apollo, being in love with Cassandra, the beautiful daughter of King Priamus of Troy, gave her a present: the ability to predict the future. When she rejected him in spite of that gift, he could not take it back because a

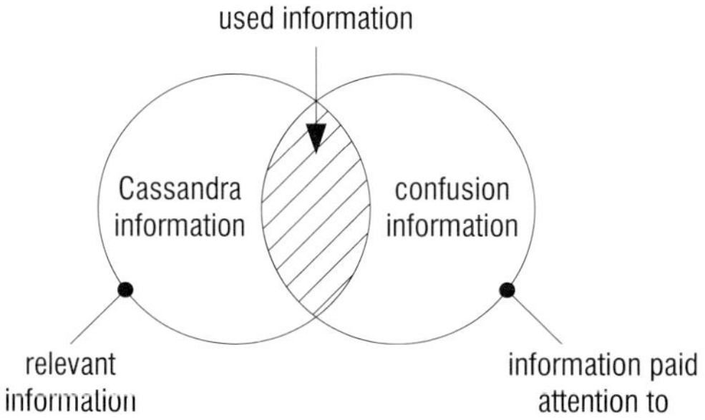

Figure 6.1 Information pertinent to managers.

gift from a god is a gift forever. Therefore, he provided her with another: no one would ever listen to her. When she warned the Trojans about the wooden horse, her advice was ignored and the city was subsequently destroyed.

The reason why available relevant information is ignored, is often its threatening nature. For the Trojans the information that the terrible war with the Greeks was not over, was simply too threatening. Other causes are:

- Poor accessibility.
- Filtering information to avoid ambiguity as described in Section 6.2.

The information paid attention to by the manager that is not relevant is called *confusion information*, as this type of information tends to confuse the issue. In dealing with information, the manager should, of course, primarily be concerned with Cassandra information. He must strive to reduce the likelihood that relevant information is overlooked or ignored.

In principle, this can be done in two different ways (Figure 6.2):

- Increasing the information paid attention to. It cannot be denied that in this way Cassandra information is indeed reduced, but at the same time confusion information increases. The availability of ever more powerful computers generates a trend in this direction (making the problem of overabundance of information worse than it was already);
- Reducing Cassandra information along with reducing confusion information. This is what good (expert) consultants try to do: telling their client what is relevant to him. No more, no less.

The latter is the essence of our typology: try to simultaneously minimize both Cassandra information and confusion information.

6.2 Filtering information to avoid ambiguity

It is human nature to dislike ambiguity and indecisiveness. As a result, people have difficulty to change their view once they have formed their opinion.

Their apparent unwillingness to face reality in the light of new information should not be seen as dishonesty. Their perception may be genuine but distorted by a process of selective filtering of information, which tends to confirm the correctness of their point-of-view or the decision taken. This phenomenon, known as *cognitive dissonance reduction*, is explained by Festinger's theory of cognitive dissonance (1957), which can be summarized as follows. A person who has to choose between two alternatives, experiences an uneasy feeling, *cognitive dissonance*. This uneasiness is stronger:

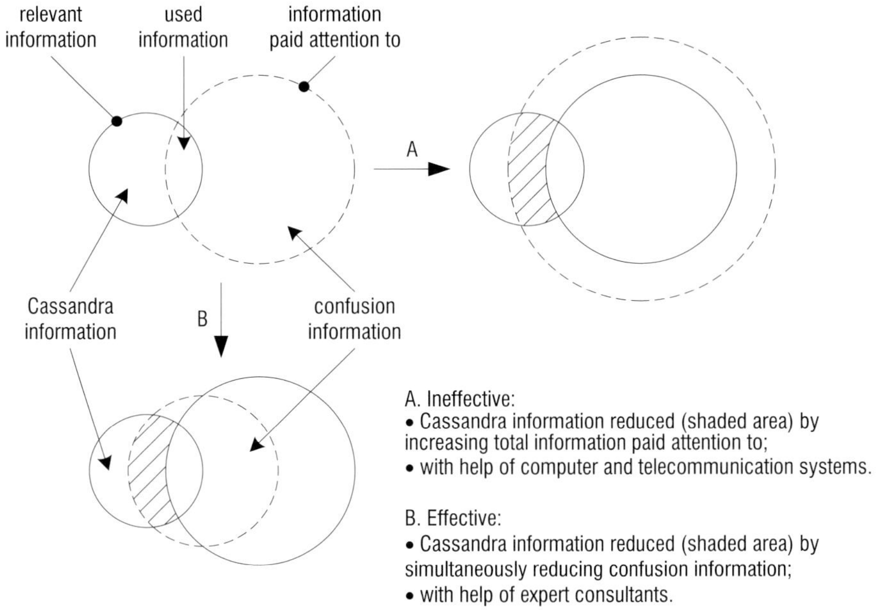

Figure 6.2 Two approaches to reducing Cassandra information.

- The more the perceived advantages and disadvantages of the two alternatives are in balance.

- The more important the matter is (e.g. to decide on another job causes more cognitive dissonance than the decision on bringing along an umbrella since it may rain or the weather may be fine).

The cognitive dissonance does not immediately disappear once the person has made up his mind. To reduce it, the person selectively absorbs information which confirms the decision made, the phenomenon of *cognitive dissonance reduction*. It explains why brochures on cars are not primarily collected by people who intend to buy a car, but by those who have just bought one! It explains why a board of directors is always reluctant to fire a managing director they once appointed. Similarly, when an operation gets the green light, the information paid attention to by the decision makers is invariably of a positive nature, making it extremely difficult to accept, at a later stage when new relevant information surfaces, the conclusion that it should be abandoned. Operation Market Garden in WWII in which the information on the presence of two SS armor divisions near Arnhem was ignored by Montgomery's staff, is a tragic example.

Table 6.1 Effective managerial approach to cope with information

Sequence:
What is relevant to my purpose?
What is available?
What is still missing?
Assumptions on relevant information that cannot be obtained.

When deliberations on a decision continue over a long period of time, the acceptance of the decision, either way, is reduced as a result of the cognitive dissonance reduction of the players involved. Awareness of the phenomenon of cognitive dissonance reduction and realization that no human being can escape its effects, can help the project manager to achieve appropriate timing of decisions.

6.3 Managerial effectiveness in handling information

In practice, we often see that managers tend to swallow whatever information reaches them (approach A of Figure 6.2). They read almost everything that arrives on their desk and attend seminars on a variety of subjects, and still their curiosity seems never to be satisfied. In their day-to-day decision-making they ask first what information is available and only secondarily what is relevant. In this way a lot of information paid attention to is confusion information which can have a paralyzing effect on the manager. This approach is, therefore, ineffective.

Effective managers place primary emphasis on what is relevant before looking at what information is available (Table 6.1).

Relevant information that cannot be obtained is taken into account by analyzing the implications of the manager's options in various scenarios. A scenario is a relevant and plausible future that cannot be controlled. A strategy is an option, a choice of a course of action, available to the decision maker.

Let us explain the concept with the example of the decision on a holiday destination. When the weather is bad, you want to visit a museum or attend a concert. When the weather is fine, you want to sport in the fresh air. But you don't know, and never will know, what the weather actually will be. Your options and their consequences in the bad-weather scenario and in the fine-weather scenario are given in Table 6.2.

You decide for option C and are prepared to pay the higher hotel price to be sure of a good holiday regardless of the weather. This is the essence of scenario planning: create, with imagination and fantasy, a strategy (option)

Table 6.2 Scenario planning for a holiday

Strategy	Scenario: Weather fine	bad
A. Resort for outdoor sports	++	−−
B. Resort for cultural activities	−−	++
C. Resort offering both (hotel being 10% more expensive)	+	+

Table 6.3 Scenario planning for an airline

Strategy	Scenario: Passenger air mile demand low	high
A. Expand: buy planes, hire pilots	−−	++
B. Consolidate: do not invest in airplanes and pilots	++	−−
C. Buy options for airplanes, offer pilots the option of a contract which provides them with a bonus for the employer's right to fire them when necessary.	+	+

yielding a satisfactory outcome in various scenarios.

For an airline, the decision to expand or to consolidate depends on the future demand of passenger airmiles. The scenario planning for this dilemma could be as given in Table 6.3.

Scenario planning has become fashionable after its successful application on a global scale by Shell. As a result, the technique tends to be associated with large organizations. The underlying principle, however, of accepting that certain relevant information simply cannot be obtained, but can nevertheless be accounted for in strategic decision making, is by no means limited to large corporations (as is illustrated in our holiday example).

7 The power game

Power plays an important role in any large complex project.

In particular, the project manager has to manage his boss who, in turn, can exercise power to help him. Peter Drucker (1977) once published an article in which its main message was completely reflected in its title: How to manage your boss? Frans provided me with a striking example. He increased the local Chinese content to a level far above what had been foreseen in the initial planning of the Nanhai project. He suspected that Western suppliers could approach Shell's top management and point out that this was irresponsible in view of the required quality. He therefore informed Shell's President in advance and explained that he had taken the necessary precautions to ensure quality. This enabled the President to react on any complaint from Western suppliers with a simple 'Thank you for the warning'.

Apparently, the project manager has to play the power game if he is to remain in function till the completion of his project.

It is useful to be aware of the different kinds of power:

Formal power Formal authority because of rank or position in the organization. 'You have to follow my order because I am your boss'.

Sanction power Being in the position to reward (positive sanction power) or to punish (negative sanction power).

Knowledge power Knowledge, being an expert, provides power. Hence the proverb 'knowledge is power'.

Reference power Power as a result of individual prominence.

Managers tend to rely primarily on formal and sanction power, consultants can only exercise knowledge and reference power.

The project manager of a large and complex project needs all four kinds of power, as will be illustrated with the examples of the sections below.

7.1 Formal power

How formal power, or rather the lack of it, can make a decisive difference for the effectiveness of a project manager is illustrated by the following example of a ship yard for offshore equipment.

First, we have to explain the difference between managing a project and managing a company.

Project management refers to managing projects, undertakings characterized by having a beginning and an end within an overseeable period of time. Best management practices for managing projects that by definition are limited in time are different from those for managing enterprises that are meant to continue, as it were, forever. To illustrate the difference, two models for building ships are contrasted:

1. Viking-model;

2. Toothpaste-model.

In the middle ages, the Vikings in Norway had a tradition that the eldest son inherited everything. The other sons were disinherited and banned. They had no other choice than to leave the country to get gold and girls overseas.

Building a boat for the overseas expedition can be seen as a project with a start and a finish. The management of that project is characterized by its ad-hoc nature and the central role of the project leader. Building a series of ships, by contrast, can be done more efficiently by focusing on the flow of materials rather than on the completion of any particular building number under construction. As with a toothpaste tube, the materials have to flow through the yard and one has to press to achieve that flow. The model for this way of building is therefore called the Toothpaste model and the model for building single items is called the Viking model. The characteristics of both models are given in Tables 7.1 and 7.2.

Which model is preferable depends on the characteristics of the objects that are being built. If the objects to be built are very different from each other, the Viking model is best. When the objects are very similar, the best efficiency is achieved by working along the lines of the Toothpaste model. For instance, large Japanese construction firms secured substantial efficiency improvements by changing to what was called 'industrial construction processes', so actually a transition from the Viking model to the Toothpaste model.

In general, the appropriateness of application shifts over time from the Viking model to the Toothpaste model (Table 7.3) but in some cases a return to the Viking model is required.

Example: *Shipyard for offshore equipment*

A newly appointed managing director of a shipyard specialized in offshore equipment: drill ships, crane ships, drilling platforms, single buoy mooring systems, etc., noticed that the yard's organization was structured along the lines of the Toothpaste model. The heads of the various departments - drawing room, purchasing department, section building, casco building, finishing, etc. -

Table 7.1 Viking model characteristics

Viking model
In the middle ages: If not eldest son → disinherited, banned → no gold, no girls Solution: make alliance with others with the same fate, build a Viking ship with them and get gold and girls from overseas Characteristics: Ad-hoc, once-only event Design adapted to individual wishes Features of a project: a start and a finish Flexible, opportunistic 'Project manager' controls progress Many variations: own or copied design, build or steal a ship

Table 7.2 Toothpaste model characteristics

Toothpaste model
Characteristics: repetitious standardization progress depending on flow of materials, controlled through system of procedures continuity (exploiting the learning curve)

Table 7.3 Appropriateness of Viking model and Toothpaste model

<table>
<tr><th></th><th>Viking model</th><th>Toothpaste model</th></tr>
<tr><td>Once-only projects</td><td>Appropriate<ul><li>information<ul><li>face-to-face</li><li>unstructured</li></ul></li><li>easy to accommodate client's individual wishes</li><li>flexible</li><li>efficient; overheads: one working foreman</li></ul></td><td>Inappropriate<ul><li>information<ul><li>lot of confusing information</li><li>emphasis on structured information, resulting in Cassandra information</li></ul></li><li>difficult to accommodate client's individual wishes</li><li>inflexible</li><li>inefficient; overheads</li></ul></td></tr>
<tr><td>Repetitious projects</td><td>Inappropriate<ul><li>information<ul><li>a lot of Cassandra information</li></ul></li><li>difficult to accommodate client's individual wishes</li><li>low quality</li><li>delivery times problematic</li><li>inefficient</li></ul></td><td>Appropriate<ul><li>information<ul><li>not face-to-face, but via drawings, documents and computers</li></ul></li><li>T-Ford principle: client's individual wishes accommodated within limits</li><li>flexibility depending on degree of automation</li><li>efficient</li></ul></td></tr>
</table>

constituted the second echelon that had considerable power. Project coordinators, assigned to individual building numbers, had a much lower status and no formal power.

As the yard had no more than five building numbers per year, the new managing director decided to restructure the organization according to the Viking model. He asked his people to explain to him the job of a project coordinator. After some rather lengthy explanation, he summarized by saying: 'I am getting the point, a project coordinator is someone with responsibility for something but without the required authority and power.' A small team was appointed to define the terms of reference for project managers, as opposed to project coordinators. Five project managers were appointed, one senior former department head and four aggressive young promising engineers from lower ranks of the organization.

The power given to the project managers came as a shock to some of the department heads. The rule was that in case of conflict the project manager's view would prevail over that of the department head who could only appeal in the next meeting of the executive board. That only happened once, when the purchasing manager did not agree to helping a subcontractor because it would make it impossible to file a claim. The project manager could show that the subcontractor's work was on the critical path: if he was too late, the delivery of the ship had to be delayed at cost much higher than any claim on the subcontractor. His decision to help the subcontractor was therefore endorsed by the executive board. Before the change to the Viking model the sub-optimal point of view of the purchasing manager would have prevailed.

Similar advantages were obtained by decisions taken by the project managers that were by contract up to the owner. For instance, if the owner had to decide on the color of the owner's cabin he would receive only one reminder from the project manager. In case of no reply, the project manager would then decide himself: 'We'll make it green!'. Before the change to the Viking model such incidents would always end up in costly delays. An even more significant improvement was achieved by conscientious recording of all changes and additions in the work that were requested by the customer. Knowing that nothing was forgotten and everything was properly recorded, the managing director could easily obtain agreement on the final billing by granting some minor concessions to the owner.

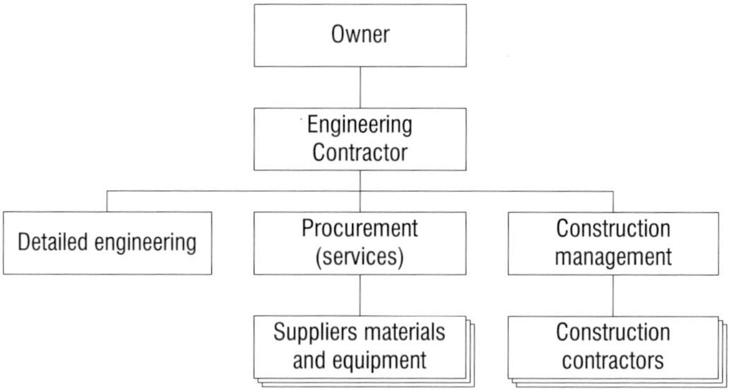

Figure 7.1 Typical project organization and work break down structure on large engineering and construction projects.

> The change to the Viking model restored the yard to profitability after years of losses.

The example clearly shows why the project manager succeeds where the project coordinator fails: lack of formal power of the latter.

7.2 Sanction power

The numerous subcontractors involved in any large, complex project are primarily interested in getting their money. Paying or not paying their bills constitutes a crucial positive or negative sanction power, which should be in the hands of the project manager if that power is to be exercised to obtain the best performance from the subcontractors.

Financial employees assigned to projects are inclined to interfere with the decision to pay or not to pay by checking themselves if the subcontractor deserves to be paid. This is highly undesirable as it undermines the power of the project manager towards the subcontractors. Keeping the subcontractors motivated is a primary task of the project manager who should therefore be empowered with the associated financial power.

In very large engineering and construction projects, the owner usually outsources the project implementation to an international engineering contractor. A typical project organization for this purpose is shown in Figure 7.1 (Berends and Dhillon, 2004; Berends, 2007). Generally, some 20% of the project implementation cost pertains directly to engineering contractor involvement, 40% to procurement from suppliers of materials and equipment, and another 40% to construction contractors.

The outsourcing of project management tasks raises the question of how to motivate the engineering contractor to work genuinely in the interest of the

owner and not opportunistically pursue his own interests. The delegation of project management tasks to the engineering contractor provides him with considerable sanction power that, preferably, should be balanced with financial sanction power from the part of the owner. Financial sanction power of the owner vis á vis the engineering contractor depends for a great deal on the type of contract between them. In a traditional 'lump sum/fixed price' contract, the project cost risk is carried by the engineering contractor, who includes a premium for this in his price. In a 'cost plus incentive fee/engineering procurement and construction management' contract, the project cost risk is carried by the owner, who generally is in a better position to do so than the engineering contractor. The resulting better balance of sanction power generates a reciprocal dependency between owner and engineering contractor at the end of the development phase of the project, providing a strong incentive for genuine collaboration and effective working together.

7.3 Knowledge power

As an example of the use of knowledge power, I describe the following incident when I was managing director of a shipyard for offshore equipment.

On the day of the launching of a drill ship, the doom message was passed on to me that the launching had to be called-off because there was not enough water in the river. The launching was scheduled to be within a few hours, so there was hardly any time for consultation. The harbor authorities had advised to postpone the launching to the next spring tide, which would mean a delay of some weeks. Also my own people advised me to do so. I then asked them to leave me alone for a moment so that I could think. My thoughts were the following:

1. Every day of delay represents a loss in the order of one hundred thousand dollars. Cancellation would entail a loss of more than a million.
2. What could happen if the water in the river would indeed be too low? The bow of the vessel would then bump on the edge of the slipway and be damaged by it. The stern with propeller would not be in any danger. We could trim the ship by ballasting the tanks in the aft body so that the damaged bow would come above the water surface. The damaged part of the bow could then be burned away and a new section welded to the hull. An operation costing no more than a hundred thousand, I estimated.

So, I decided to launch the ship as planned. The people who had advised me to cancel the launching were appalled: 'This decision is your personal responsibility,' to which I replied, 'Yes, it is.' Etc. The launching then took place without any damage.

How could I be so sure and decide against all available advice? I had sufficient knowledge about ships to make that decision without having to rely on the advice of other people. Similarly, a manager of a large, complex construction project cannot function properly without the knowledge required for estimating technical risks.

7.4 Reference power

The manager of a large complex project will inevitably encounter situations in which relying on his reference power is his last resort. A situation in which he can only say: 'Please do this, because I beg you'.

In getting funds for an R&D project, which is by nature risky and uncertain, the best argument often is: 'I like it so much'. That means to rely on your reference power.

The power of great political leaders, like for instance Charles de Gaulle and Nelson Mandela, is largely based on their reference power. It is the most important of the four kinds of power. It makes all the difference between people who get things done and those who do not.

7.5 Acceptance of the stakeholder-oriented approach

The stakeholder-oriented managerial approach will not be welcomed with applause by everyone. Many will doubt its effectiveness, particularly when they were brought up in a 'macho' culture, such as when their native country scores highly on the culture dimension Masculinity according to Hofstede (2001). Some countries which have a rather high score on this dimension are listed in Table 7.4. Countries with a more feminine – caring – culture, as becomes apparent from their low scores on Masculinity, are listed in Table 7.5. As a corollary, acceptance of the stakeholder-oriented approach will be a lot more problematic in the countries of Table 7.4 than those of Table 7.5.

In the Nanhai project the predominantly Dutch project management team had enough power to enforce the stakeholder-oriented approach, because they had the blessing to do so from both the CEO of the project and the president of their corporation. The formal power of the highest level is essential for the acceptance of the stakeholder-oriented managerial approach.

Table 7.4 Countries scoring high on Masculinity.

Country	Score
Slovakia*	110
Japan	95
Hungary*	88
Austria	79
Venezuela	73
Italy	70
Switzerland	70
Mexico	69
Ireland	68
Jamaica	68
China*	66
Germany	66
Great Britain	66
Colombia	64
Philippines	64
Poland*	64
Ecuador	63
South Africa	63
United States	62
Australia	61
Mean	50
Standard deviation	20

* estimated

Table 7.5 Countries scoring low on Masculinity.

Country	Score
Finland	26
Costa Rica	21
Denmark	16
Netherlands	14
Norway	8
Sweden	5
Mean	50
Standard deviation	20

Epilogue

Every project is unique in the sense that certain features of it cannot be recognized in other projects. The issues associated with these unique features have to be pro-actively addressed with the concept of the key issues matrix in which these issues are identified along with ways to resolve them.

Issues related to common features of projects can be resolved using general tools and concepts. It is up to the project manager to decide which ones to include in his repertoire: only the control-oriented concepts recommended in the main stream of project management literature or also the stakeholder-oriented concepts described here. The latter will increase his effectiveness in the long term, but in the short term he may be faced with an acceptance problem because his approach may be perceived as soft and inefficient. He will feel like a tennis player who sees his chances of winning initially reduced when he adopts a new, in the long run better, tennis grip.

Hopefully, this book will then help him to hold on and persevere in a truly stakeholder-oriented attitude.

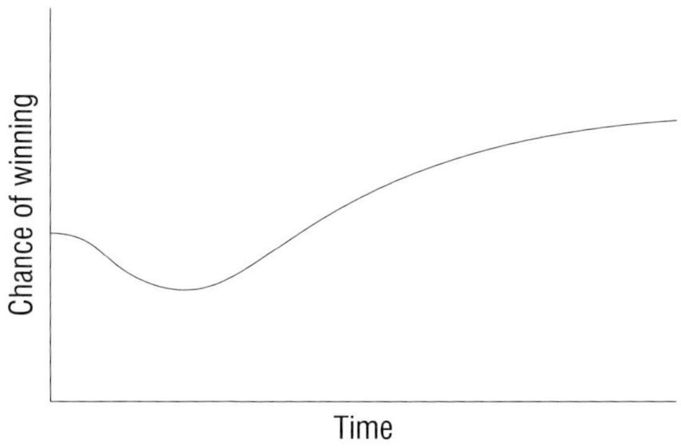

Adopting a new tennis grip.

A Appendix to Chapter 4: Risk ranking in probabilistic network planning

This appendix, taken from Binnekamp et al. (2006, pp. 245-258), describes the state-of-the-art of probabilistic network planning without allowance for mitigations on the run, but including our new concept of risk ranking.

The current state-of-the-art of decision modelling for construction projects is characterised by the following three techniques, which are widely in use:

1. Gantt or bar chart, which shows the start and finish times of the project's activities.
2. Critical Path Method (CPM), which allows the interdependence of the activities to be taken into account, and the identification of the Critical Path of subsequent activities in which any delay in an activity causes a delay in the total project duration.
3. Program Evaluation and Review Technique (PERT), which is similar to CPM, but allows estimated probability distributions for the duration of the activities to be accounted for.

CPM was developed by Kelly and Walker in 1957. PERT originates from the Special Projects Office of the U.S. Navy and was developed in the late fifties for the Polaris missile program.

The Gantt chart is most frequently used because of its simplicity, but does not show the relationships between the activities that are needed to complete the project (Fig. A.1).

CPM is better for the larger and more complex jobs in that the network shows the interdependence of the various operations (Fig. A.2).

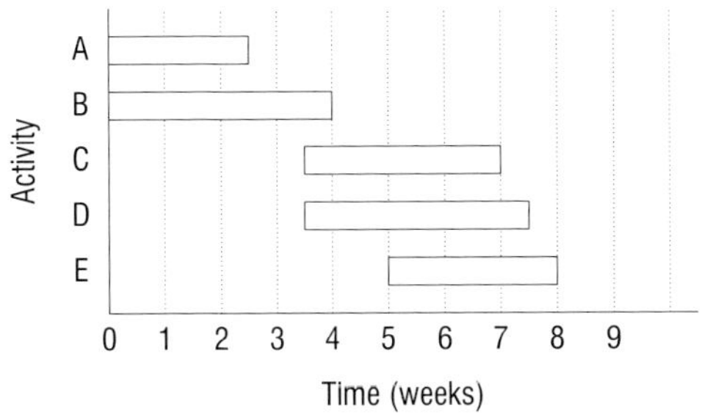

Figure A.1 Example GANTT chart

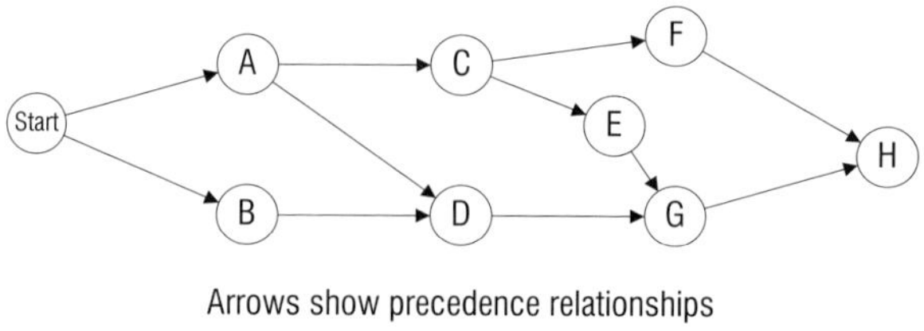

Figure A.2 Example CPM

The initial real-life experiences with CPM in manufacturing scheduling were disappointing, in that actual project durations tended to considerably exceed the predictions according to the model. The variability in expected activity times had to be accounted for. In its simplest form, this can be done by adding an estimated margin to each expected activity time, to allow for unforeseen delays.

PERT is similar to CPM, but it allows three estimates for the duration of an activity to be provided: a pessimistic, a best guess and an optimistic estimate.

In this appendix we will first describe the traditional critical path method, the probabilistic approach of PERT, and Monte Carlo simulation on a priori selected paths through the network, which represent the current state-of-the-art. We will then show how to conduct Monte Carlo simulation without any a priori selection of paths through the network. Subsequently, the concept of path ranking is introduced in two different rankings: slack (or float) ranking and risk ranking. The latter is to be preferred for large and complex projects.

A.1 Deterministic network planning: CPM

Modelling a construction planning using LP software is in essence no more than translating the (graphical) relations between the different activities into mathematical equations. The relation between two activities in a construction planning can easily be translated into a mathematical formula. We will restrain ourselves to Finish-to-Start relations with a relation-duration of zero. In the critical path method the activity-duration is considered invariable.

Consider the part of an AON* construction planning shown in Figure A.3.

This Finish-to-Start relationship means that activity B cannot start earlier than the earliest finish of activity A. In a mathematical equation:

$$x_1 \geq x_2 \tag{A.1}$$

*Of the two approaches for representing a network, Activity On Node (AON) and Activity On Arrow (AOA), the former is most commonly used because of its clarity and possibilities. The nodes are rectangles representing activities, the arrows represent the relationships.

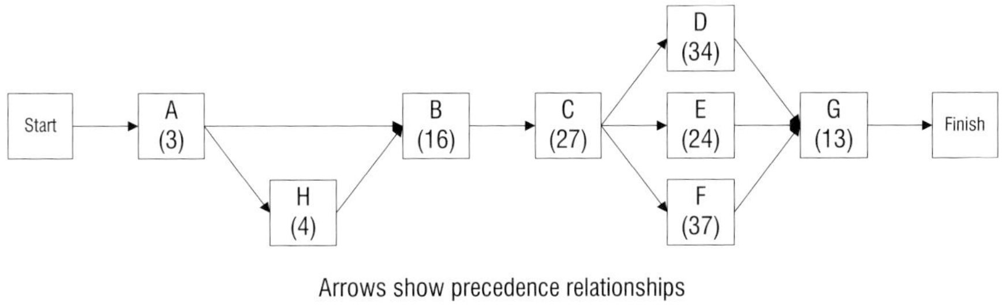

Figure A.3 Illustration of part of a construction planning

where x_1 represents the earliest start of activity B and x_2 represents the earliest finish of activity A. We know the duration of activity A so the equation can be rewritten as:

$$x_1 \geq x_2 + b_1 \tag{A.2}$$

where x_1 represents the earliest start of activity B and x_2 represents the earliest start of activity A and b_1 represents the duration of activity A. This equation can be rewritten as:

$$x_1 - x_2 \geq b_1 \tag{A.3}$$

This equation follows the standard form of a constraint from an LP model:

$$\text{Maximise} \quad Z = \sum_{j=1}^{n} c_j x_j \tag{A.4}$$

subject to:

$$\sum_{j=1}^{n} a_{ij} x_j \leq b_i \qquad \text{for } i = 1, 2, \ldots, m$$

and

$$x_j \geq 0 \qquad \text{for } j = 1, 2, \ldots, n$$

In critical path planning we are interested in the shortest total project duration. So the objective function is to minimise the total project duration. We will explain this using the following example.

Consider a simple network planning with two parallel activities A and B. Activity A has a duration of 5 days and activity B has a duration of 3 days. The Start and Finish activities are artificial activities that define the project's start and the project's finish. We want to build a model to calculate the shortest project duration. This simple example is just to illustrate the modelling of a critical path planning.

We use the modelling ABC to build the LP model in Excel:

	A	B	C	D	E	F	G	H
1	Endogenous variables	ES_ST	ES_A	ES_B	ES_FI			
2	Outcome	0	0	0	0			

Figure A.4 Defining 'Adjustable' cells

	A	B	C	D	E	F	G	H
1	Endogenous variables	ES_ST	ES_A	ES_B	ES_FI			
2	Outcome	0	0	0	0			
3								
4	Objective function	-1			1	0		

Figure A.5 Defining 'Best' cell

A. Define the 'Adjustable' cells. In this case these are the earliest start dates of the different activities, following Figure A.4. The cells B2 through E2 hold the adjustables.

B. Define the 'Best' cell. This would be the total project duration given the earliest start dates of the different activities. In Excel we create the entries following Figure A.5, where cell F4 is the cell that needs to be minimised.

   This might be confusing so we will explain this in more detail. The total project duration equals the earliest start of the artificial start-activity subtracted from the earliest start of the artificial finish-activity:

$$Z = -x_1 + x_4 \tag{A.5}$$

   where x_1 represents the earliest start of the artificial start-activity and x_4 represents the earliest start of the artificial finish-activity. Cell F4 must be the outcome of B4 times B2 added to the outcome of C4 times C2 added to the outcome of D4 times D2 added to the outcome of E4 times E2 or in mathematical terms:

$$Z = c_1x_1 + c_2x_2 + \cdots + c_nx_n \tag{A.6}$$

   In Excel, using the sumproduct function, we type in cell F4:

```
=sumproduct(B$2:E$2;B4:E4)
```

C. Define the 'Constraints' that have to be met. These are the restrictions that represent the relationships between the different activities. In Excel we create the entries following Figure A.6.

	A	B	C	D	E	F	G	H
1	Endog. var.	ES_ST	ES_A	ES_B	ES_FI			
2	Outcome	0	0	0	0			
3								
4	Objective f.	-1			1	0		
5						required		available
6	St FS A	-1	1			0	>=	0
7	St FS B	-1		1		0	>=	0
8	A FS Fi		-1		1	0	>=	5
9	B FS Fi			-1	1	0	>=	3

Figure A.6 Defining 'Constraints'

These are in fact representations of the following mathematical equation:

$$a_{11}x_1 + a_{12}x_2 + \cdots + a_{1n}x_n \leq b_1 \tag{A.7}$$

Row 8 states for instance that the artificial finish-activity cannot start earlier than the earliest start of activity A added with the duration of activity A:

$$x_4 \geq x_2 + 5 \tag{A.8}$$

Where x_4 represents the earliest start of the artificial finish-activity, x_2 the earliest start of activity A and 5 equals the duration of activity A. We can rewrite this equation to meet the standard matrix layout:

$$x_4 - x_2 \geq 5 \tag{A.9}$$

Note that the formula created in cell F4 can be copied into cells F6 to F9. All other cells contain no formulas, just values entered.

The model is now ready to be solved. Figure A.7 shows a screenshot of the actual solved model. As you can see the minimal project duration is 5 days.

A.2 Probabilistic network planning: PERT

PERT allows three estimates for the duration of an activity to be provided: a most pessimistic estimate (p), a most likely estimate (m) and a most optimistic estimate (o). When using PERT, it is usually assumed that activity times follow the beta probability distribution (Fig. A.8).

With two more assumptions — total project completion times follow a normal distribution and activity times are stochastically independent — answers

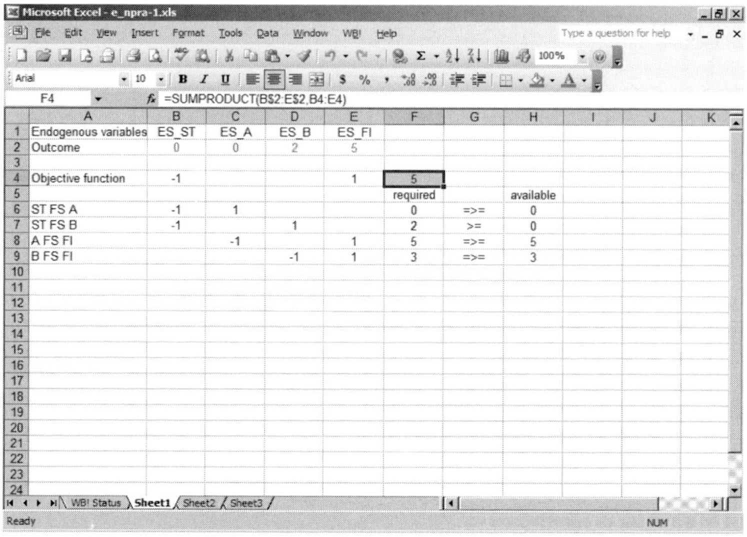

Figure A.7 Screenshot of solved model

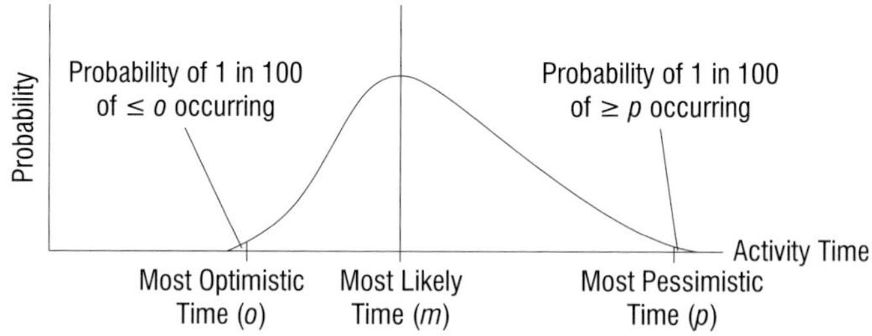

Figure A.8 Beta probability distribution with three estimates can then be given to questions regarding the probability of finishing the project on time. For more detailed information on CPM and PERT, reference is made to Render et al. (2003) Chapter 7 and Hargitay and Yu (1993) Chapter 8.

The probabilistic approach of PERT constitutes an improvement compared to the deterministic CPM approach, but it brings along a fundamental shortcoming: it only provides information on activities on the Critical Path that was established using the expected mean times (m) of the activities the project is composed of. It may very well be, that the Critical Path for achieving, say, a 90% probability of completion before the end date of that path, is different from the one calculated with the estimated means of the activities.

A.3 Risk assessment in network planning through Monte Carlo simulation

As a solution for this problem, Lanza (2003) proposes a Monte Carlo approach. In essence, this involves the following steps:

1. Establish most optimistic/most likely/most pessimistic estimates for the duration of all project activities;

2. Calculate the Critical Path using the most-likely-estimates. So far the procedure is the same as in traditional PERT planning;

3. Establish one or more other paths through the network that may actually become critical paths as a result of high variability in the duration of activities in those paths;

4. Conduct a Monte Carlo simulation on each of these paths.

The resulting probability distributions for the project duration according to these paths provide answers to relevant questions related to the risk involved, such as:

1. Which project duration can be achieved with a 90% probability and what is the associated path of activities through the network?

2. What is the probability of meeting the deadline for completion of the project as required by the financing party and what is the associated path of activities through the network?

In both cases the critical path may be different from the Critical Path calculated with the most-likely-estimates. The Monte Carlo approach constitutes an improvement over the traditional CPM and PERT techniques because it provides additional information that is relevant to both the project manager and the financing stakeholder. The project manager's attention is drawn to activities that are not on the Critical Path but nevertheless may become critical and the financing stakeholder gets an estimate of the probability of financing problems due to a substantial delay in project completion.

The Monte Carlo approach proposed by Lanza leaves, however, one important question unanswered: Are the considered paths through the network really the most relevant ones?

When the network is extensive and complicated, a path of (statistically) critical activities could easily be overlooked. This difficulty can be avoided by applying Monte Carlo simulation in such a way that (statistically) critical paths are identified in a systematic way. This is achieved by conducting Monte Carlo simulation on the entire project instead of on one path of the network only.

A.4 The concept of path ranking

We define two different rankings of relevant paths through the network:

- Slack (or float) ranking;
- Risk ranking.

Slack ranking

Keeping in mind that other paths through the network than the Critical Path calculated with the most-likely-estimates may become critical when variability of activity durations is accounted for, we define the following paths:

1. Primary Path. This is the Critical Path calculated with the most-likely-estimates. The slack (or float) of the activities on this path is zero.
2. Secondary Path. This is the path with the least total slack compared to the Critical Path.
3. Tertiary Path. This is the path which has the least total slack after the Secondary Path.

This ranking will be referred to as *slack ranking*. The Secondary Path follows from the dual values (shadow prices) as described in Binnekamp et al. (2006, pp. 65-75). By removing the slack from the Secondary Path, it becomes part of the Critical Path. The dual values then identify the Tertiary Path.

Risk ranking

If the slack in the secondary and tertiary paths is small and the variability of activity durations substantially more than in the primary path, the secondary and tertiary paths may become more relevant to project control than the primary path. In other words: if variability of activity durations is taken into account, a ranking of the various paths can be established reflecting the risk involved. We will call this the *risk ranking* of the various paths of the network. The risk ranking and the associated risks are found in the following way.

For all activities the project is composed of, three estimates are made for the duration of the activity concerned: a most pessimistic, a most likely (best guess) and a most optimistic estimate. The pessimistic and optimistic estimates are defined as having a 10% probability of being exceeded. Whenever an activity duration is estimated in this way, a skewed probability distribution, such as the beta distribution, is assumed through the three given estimates. The Monte Carlo simulation is then conducted by carrying out a critical path calculation, say, 2 000 times, using activity durations that are obtained from the skewed distributions (by drawing a random number which is corrected for the skewed distribution). The frequency distribution of the 2 000 calculations provides the probability distribution for the duration of the entire project. A counter keeps track of how many times (out of the 2 000) a given path through the network was the critical path. This provides the risk ranking of the paths and the associated risks, that is, the likelihood that they will be the critical path in reality.

As is shown in Binnekamp et al. (2006, pp. 325-327), the path ranking on slack can be very different from the path ranking on risk (frequency of being the critical path in the Monte Carlo simulation).

The risk ranking of the paths, with their associated risks, is important to the project manager as it indicates how much attention should be paid to monitoring activities on the various paths. The probability distribution for the completion of the entire project is, of course, of great interest to the financial stakeholder.

A.5 Numerical examples

Two numerical examples serve to illustrate the methodology and associated software:

1. The example from Lanza's paper (slightly adapted);
2. An actual case from the construction industry.

Example from Lanza's paper

Figure A.9 shows the network Lanza used in his paper.

In this network there are two paths, Path 1 (St-Q-R-S-Fi) and Path 2 (St-P-T-Fi). Table A.1 shows the minimum duration required anyway for each activity and three margin estimates:

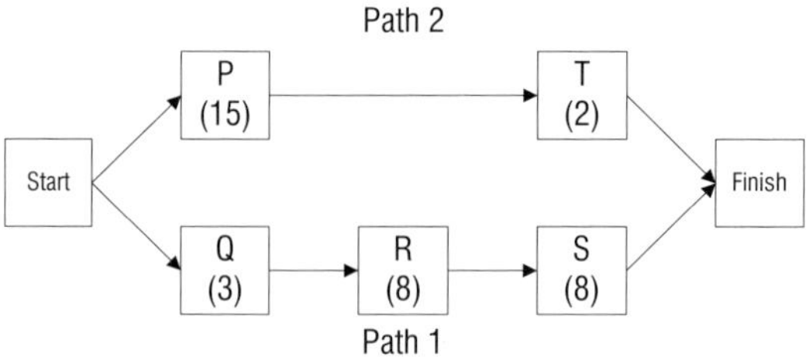

Figure A.9 Network planning of Lanza example

Table A.1 Input for the Monte Carlo simulation

Task	Minimum Duration	Optimistic Margin	Expected Margin	Pessimistic Margin	Path 1	Path 2
P	12	0	1	13		13
Q	2	0	1	2	3	
R	4	1	4	5	8	
S	5	1	3	5	8	
T	1	0	1	11		2
Total					19	15

- A most likely estimate (best guess) for the required margin on top of the minimum duration;
- A most pessimistic estimate for that margin, defined as having a 10% probability of being exceeded;
- A most optimistic estimate for that margin, defined also as having a 10% probability of being achieved.

Calculating with the minimum durations and most likely required margins (best guesses), Path 1 turns out to be the Critical Path (Primary Path). Activities on this path would get the most attention from the project manager. Activities on Path 2 (Secondary Path) would get less attention because, based upon this calculation, this path has 2 weeks more slack than the Critical Path.

The results of a Monte Carlo simulation carried out for Path 1 and Path 2 separately, according to the approach from Lanza, are given in Figure A.10 and Figure A.11 respectively.

If only Path 1 (Primary Path) is considered, the financial stakeholder, who requires an 80% probability of meeting the completion deadline, would be advised to base the financing on a project duration of 20.4 weeks. If Path 2 (Secondary Path) is also considered, the financing should be based on a duration of 22.0 weeks.

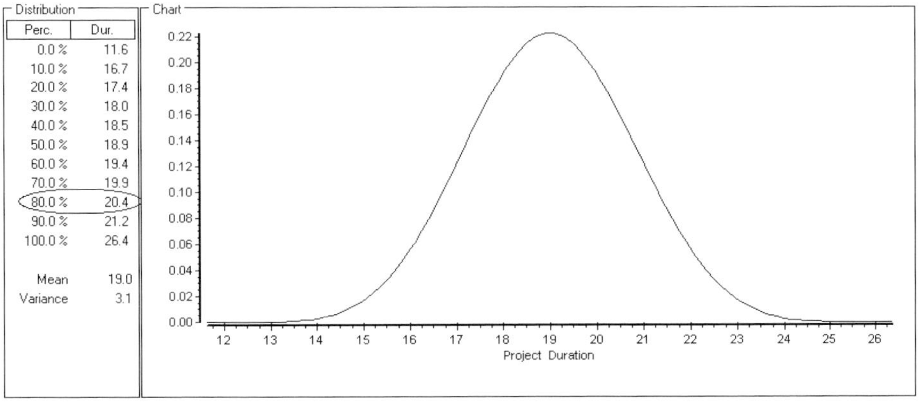

Figure A.10 Output of Monte Carlo simulation (Lanza example): probability distribution of total project duration for Path 1

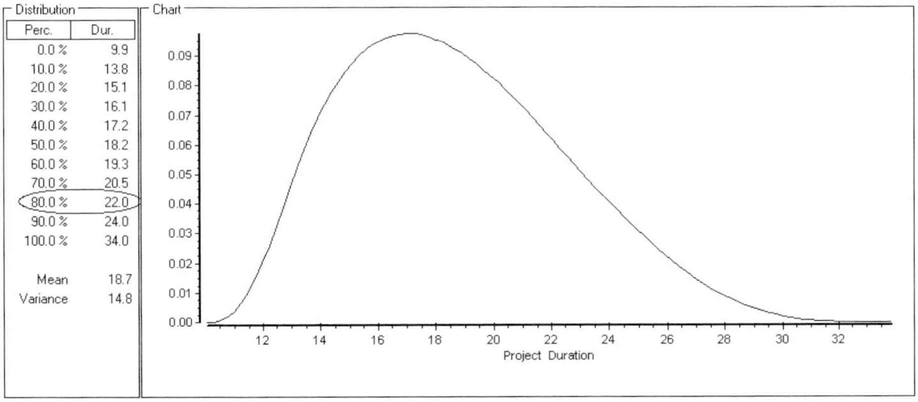

Figure A.11 Output of Monte Carlo simulation (Lanza example): probability distribution of total project duration for Path 2

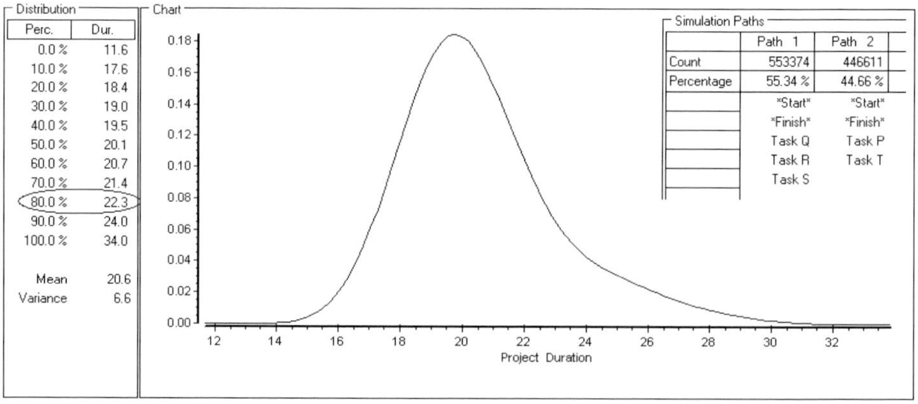

Figure A.12 Output of Monte Carlo simulation (Lanza example): probability distribution of total project duration and frequencies of occurrence in the simulation of primary and secondary paths

A Monte Carlo simulation with our new methodology results in a probability distribution of the total project duration as presented in Figure A.12.

The graph shows the distribution of the project durations derived from all Monte Carlo runs. The column in the left side of the graph shows the probability of completing the project in the associated completion time. In this example, an 80% probability is associated with a completion time of 22.3 weeks. In this simple case the difference with the aforementioned Path 2 of Lanz's example is, admittedly, small. In more complicated cases, however, the difference can be significant, in particular when a relevant secondary or tertiary path remains unidentified.

The output also gives the frequencies of occurrence of the Primary and Secondary Paths in the Monte Carlo simulation. As can be seen from the 'Percentage' row under 'Simulation Paths', Path 1 (St-Q-R-S-Fi) was critical in 55% of all runs whereas Path 2 (St-P-T-Fi) was critical 45% of all runs. The latter means that the Secondary Path 2, although still second in the risk ranking, has a probability as high as 45% of being critical in reality. This constitutes important information for the project manager, who gets a warning to pay appropriate attention to monitoring the activities on Path 2.

From the probability distribution for the completion of the entire project Figure A.12 the financial stakeholder can see that the project has a probability of 80% of being completed within 22.3 weeks, which means that the financing should be based on a 22.3 week project duration, and not on 20.4 weeks as follows from the traditional PERT calculation.

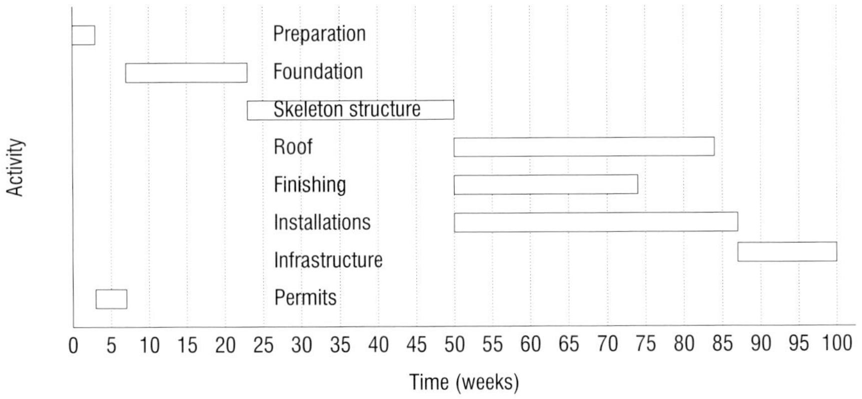

Figure A.13 GANTT chart of construction industry example

Table A.2 Input for the Monte Carlo simulation

Task	Minimum Duration	Optimistic Margin	Expected Margin	Pessimistic Margin	Path A	Path B	Path C
A	2	0	1	2	3	3	3
B	15	0	1	4	16	16	16
C	25	0	2	5	27	27	27
D	30	0	4	10	34		
E	22	0	2	4		24	
F	34	0	3	7			37
G	12	0	1	2	13	13	13
H	3	0	1	4	4	4	4
Total					97	87	100

Example from the construction industry

Our second example is a simplified actual case from the construction industry. Figure A.13 presents the Gantt chart of the project planning. Table A.2 shows the minimum duration required anyway for each activity and three estimates for the required margin. The network planning of the activities is given in Figure A.14. The output of the Monte Carlo simulation according to our new methodology is given in Figure A.15.

The frequency of the Secondary Path being critical in the Monte Carlo simulation is significant: 29%. This means that, in the later stages of the project, the project manager should not only pay attention to activity F (installations) on the Primary (Critical) Path, but also to activity D (roof) on the Secondary Path. If the financial stakeholder requires an 80% probability of completion on time, the project financing should be based on a 106.5 week project duration.

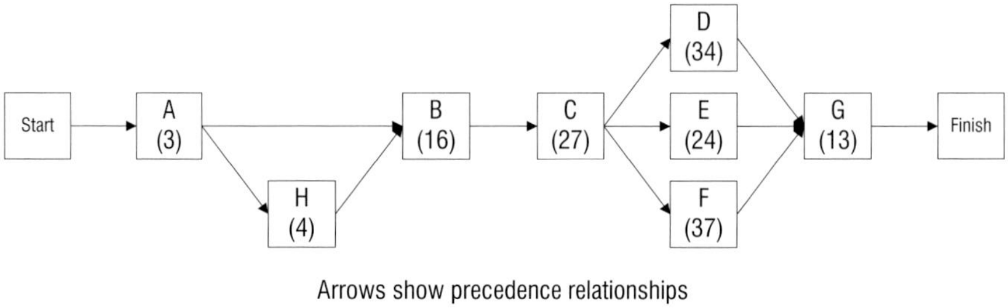

Figure A.14 Network planning of construction industry example

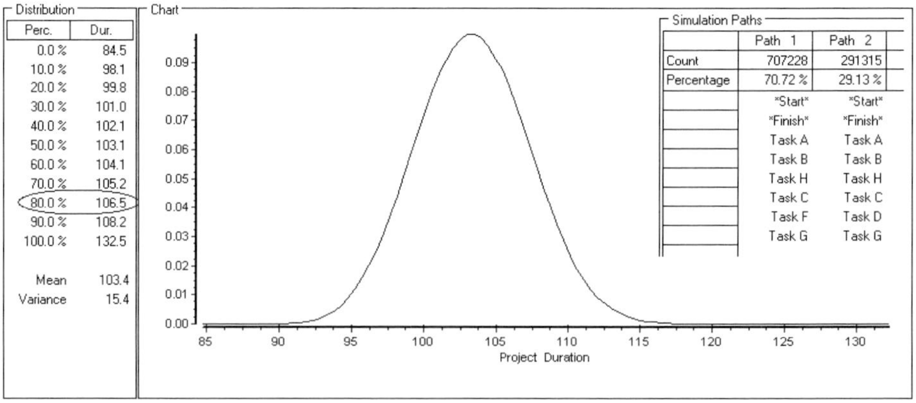

Figure A.15 Output of Monte Carlo simulation (construction industry example)

B Case: Ruta del Sol

B.1 Project description "Ruta del Sol"

Colombia

Colombia is a country in South America. It is bordered to five other countries (Brazil, Venezuela, Ecuador, Peru and Panama) and two oceans (Atlantic and Pacific). It has a total area of 1,138,914 km2 and almost 46 million inhabitants. Colombia is the country with the largest cumulative growth in Latin America since 2001 and it had a real annual growth of 7.7% in 2007. The currency used is the Peso*.

To increase the mobility in Colombia, the state wants to increase accessibility by initiating the project *Ruta del Sol*. Ruta del Sol means "Route to the Sun", chosen because it connects the centre of the country with the sunny beaches of the Caribbean Sea. Cartagena (in the north of Colombia) has recently become an international port for cruisers and the widening of the Panama Canal will make the area a bigger hub for global market transactions.

The Project

The project Ruta del Sol consists of a corridor that stretches over more than 1,000 kilometers. It will connect the capital of Colombia, Bogota, with north Caribbean coast. By doing this it crosses nine Departments of Colombia, these Departments have major urban centers, large agricultural, industrial or mining areas. The concession of the project was started in 2008. The construction will start in 2010 and should be finished in 2020.

The project is divided into three tranches, two tranches (2 and 3) that need to be upgraded and one tranche (1) that needs to be built new. The three tranches are visualized in Figure B.1.

Tranche 1 heads from Puerto Salgar to El Korán, the length of the new road is 78 km. The new road will reduce distance between Bogota and the Magdalena river (the main waterway in Colombia) by 25 km and approximately one hour. Because this part of Colombia is not flat, three tunnels are needed. The new road should be built within four to five years.

Tranche 2 is an already existing road that heads from Puerto Salgar to San Roque and has a length of 528 km. This road needs to be upgraded to increase the accessibility of some important production centers in that area. The upgrade should be finished in seven years.

*One US dollar is 1,897.50 Colombian Pesos, exchange rate at March 6th 2010

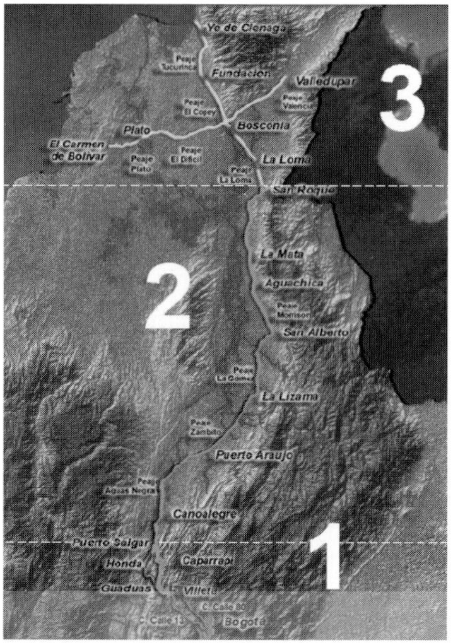

Figure B.1 The three tranches of the Ruta del Sol.

Tranche 3 is an already existing network in the north of Colombia, it consists of four roads with a total length of 465 km. The centre of the network is Bosconia. In this area the agricultural activity is really important and the new road will make the area better accessible. The road needs to be upgraded within seven years.

All the three tranches are toll roads, at the moment the annual toll revenue is US$ 70 million, this is without the new road being built. The toll is part of the payments for the consortia who are executing the tranches.

Some facts and figures of the project are summarized in Table B.1.

Table B.1 The facts and figures of the project.

Land area of Colombia	1,138,914 km2
Inhabitants of Colombia	46 million (2009)
Project investment	US$ 2.6 billion
Total length of the infrastructure	1071.3 kilometers
Traffic	11,500 vehicles per day
Toll revenue	US$ 70 million a year
Realization phase	10 years

Project organization

The four most important parties in the project are the following.

- Instituto de Nacional de Concesiones (INCO)

  INCO is a national public organization who is working on behalf of the Ministrio de Transporte (Ministry of Transport). By involving private capital they seek to develop integrated and sustainable infrastructural concessions of the country in order to optimize network infrastructure and promote national integration and competitiveness.

- International Finance Centre (IFC)

  IFC is the private arm of the World Bank Group. There are 182 countries connected with IFC. Their goal is to promote open and competitive markets in developing countries, supporting companies and mobilizing sources of finance for private enterprise development. It helps by offering developing-impact solutions by firm-level interventions.

- Ministerio de Transporte (MdT)

  Minsterio de Transporte is de governmental department which takes care of the infrastructural projects in Colombia. Their mission is to contribute to the improvement of the quality of life in Colombia by making a good infrastructural network.

- Instituto Nacional de Vias (INVIAS)

  INVIAS is working on behalf of the Ministerio de Transporte to manage the roads in Colombia. INCO helps INVIAS with the concessions, INVIAS has the knowledge of the infrastructure and INCO has the knowledge of concession making.

The government of Colombia has initiated the project through INCO, INCO made an agreement with IFC to structure the project with private participation. INVIAS is taking care of the technical side. In Figure B.2 the structure is visualized.

Moment in time

For all the three tranches studies on engineering, traffic, social and land acquisition and environment are completed. At the moment (2010) two out of three tranches are awarded (tranche 1 and 2), the third tranche is being awarded in June 2010.

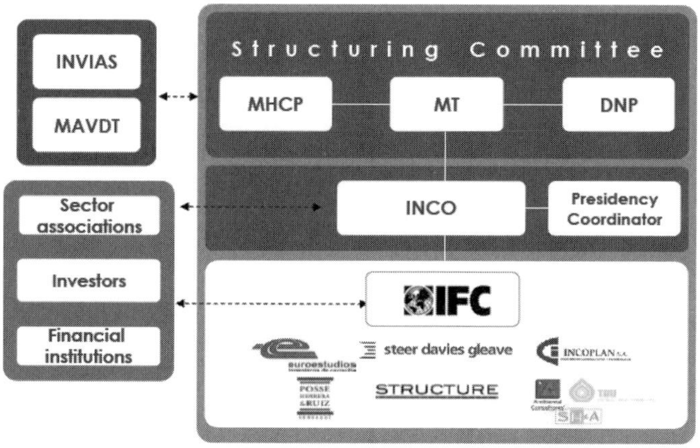

Figure B.2 The organizational structure of the project.

B.2 PI and PII aspects

Looking at the size of the project Ruta del Sol, it can be seen that it is a very large and complex project. According to Van Gunsteren (2011) this can best be done with a PII approach in combination with a PI approach. The project should be addressed with PII management, the less complex activities should be addressed with PI management. For a successful project, it is important to mix both approaches appropriately.

In this section the ten aspects regarding the literature are assessed against the practices used in the project. The ten aspects are categorized in three issues: process related, information handling related, and structure related.

Process related issues

The process related issues are the issues that determine the quality and adaptability of the process. This issue is subdivided into the following aspects:

- Goals setting (PI & PII)

  Within the Terms of Reference was room for alternative proposals, INCO even made precautions in order to prevent other bidders from adopting that alternative design and improving it or realizing it within a lower budget. INCO is attracting bidders to come up with an alternative proposal based on the preliminary design made by INCO. This shows a combination of PI and PII management. The preliminary design is PI management and the room for alternative proposals is PII management.

The first goal was to award the whole project (all the 1,000 km) to one consortium, but because of the economic crisis this became unfeasible. That is why they divided the project into three tranches, but it was still possible to bid on all the three tranches. This shows PII management, because INCO adjusted the scope of the project according to new insights.

- Leadership (PII)

  Because of the size of the project, it is difficult to manage the whole project by one organization. That is why INCO hired other organizations like IFC and Steer Davies Gleave to get in the expertise required for the project. Next to this, they also teamed up with some most important stakeholders like Ministry of Transport, Environmental Groups and INVIAS. By hiring other organizations, INCO shared some his leading power with the other stakeholders. This can be seen as PII management.

- Conflict resolution (PI)

  Even though INCO engaged several stakeholders during the awarding phase, it focussed on the most powerful stakeholders. Like other major projects in Colombia, Ruta del Sol presents a conflict resolution aspect based on power. The Terms of References and draft contracts clearly identify INCO at the top of the power structure and put the rest of the stakeholders at a weaker stance when it comes to conflict resolutions. These characteristics can be seen as PI management.

- Design process (PII)

  As mentioned in the goal setting aspect, INCO developed a preliminary design. Within this design it was possible for bidders to come up with alternative proposals. This shows that INCO was not focussing on a solution point, but made a solution space. Bidders were able to move within this solution space to come up with a solution. The PI management is included by having a preliminary design and the PII management by alternative designs.

  To control the project, INCO stated that every one percent completion is a milestone. This means that the there is some flexibility in the design process and that the project development is not framed into strict deadlines. Looking at the literature, this is PII management.

Information handling related issues

These issues are determining how information is gathered, shared and used. They are assessed by the following aspects.

- Communication (PII)

  Because it is a large project, a lot of stakeholders are affected by the decisions made by INCO. That is why INCO organized several consultation rounds in order to inform the locals and collect other insights.

  By making all the information related to the process public, everybody who was interested in the project could gather the information. This is characterized as a transparent communication and can be seen as PII management. The project presented significant changes during these consultation rounds, this shows that INCO uses this information for decision making. This is also one of the aspects of PII management.

- Persuasion of players (PII)

  INCO gave open and clear information about the performance of the existing toll plazas. This information shows the real statistics of the infrastructure and provides the bidders with honest information, which is relevant to them. For example, the third tranche has low toll revenues and this caused only one consortium to bid on it. INCO could have also chosen not to provide that information, but this would have been misleading. This aspect can be categorized as PII management.

- Progress control (PI)

  Every month there is a calculation of the Global Construction Works Index (GWCI), this calculates the amount of work that has been done. In order to set up milestones, INCO stated that every 1% of increase in the GCWI is a milestone. These milestones are used to fulfil the payments, the payments are equal to the portion of work done. This can be considered as a PI practice.

Structure related issues

The structure of a project is one of the three issues that is crucial for the success of the project. The following aspects determine what kind of structure is used.

- Division of tasks (PII)

  As mentioned, INCO involved INVIAS and IFC in the project. IFC has the expertise of the financial aspects of a project, INVIAS has the expertise on the engineering side. INCO itself has the expertise on how to manage concession projects. This clearly shows a division of tasks based on roles and is PII management. INCO also gave the responsibility of those aspects to IFC and INVIAS and held the responsibility for the concessions.

Table B.2 Summary of the ten aspects used to determine the style of management.

Aspect	Management style
Process related issues	
Goal setting	PI & PII
Leadership	PII
Conflict resolution	PI
Design process	PII
Information handling related issues	
Communication	PII
Persuasion of players	PII
Progress control	PI
Structure related issues	
Division of tasks	PII
Integration and coordination of tasks	PI
Standardization	PII

- Integration and coordination of tasks (PI)

  The integration of tasks was not done by the different roles, but mainly by INCO which always leaves room for white spots and the robustness of the process. This is considered as PI management and could be considered a weakness for a project of this scale. A PII management style could have been more suitable because the integration of tasks would have been done cooperatively by IFC, INVIAS and INCO. This would leave less room for white spots and unexpected problems.

- Standardization (PII)

  A standardized way of managing concession projects in Colombia would have resulted in a tender of the whole project instead of three separate projects. When that way of tendering would lead to no reasonable bids, they would have made minor adjustments in the ToR and tendered the whole project again resulting in a higher risk project. INCO decided to divide the whole project and split up the risk, which is a not standardized way of tendering concessions.

  Another example is the risk allocation in the project. Risks are allocated evenly between client and concessionaire. These two examples show that a PII management was used by INCO.

Table B.2 summarizes the management style practices identified.

In addition to these ten aspects, there are four extra aspects which are crucial for the success of a project and are characterized as PII management. One of these is the ability to turn problems into opportunities. Within the project it can be seen that INCO managed to do this, in the sense that they encouraged a strategic and highly complex project, despite of the global economic situation, that would lead Colombia to a more competitive place in the region.

The three most important parties were committed to a common cause, the prosperity and competitiveness of Colombia. IFC is trying to realize that within the financial possibilities, INVIAS by improving the mobility between the centre and the north regions of Colombia. INCO is trying to increase the prosperity and competitiveness of Colombia by implementing new way of contracting for large infrastructure projects. These values were used by INCO to promote a strong team building around the project.

B.3 Preference Measurements

The tendering process of the Ruta del Sol project is based on a set of comprehensive Terms of Reference (ToR) that seek to select the best proposals to award the final contract. Contrary to previous public projects that were constantly contracted out to the lowest-price bidder, the Ruta del Sol project is to be awarded following a multi-criteria selection process. This practice shows that at least in this matter, INCO adopted a PII-like management approach.

This chapter will explain what those selection criteria were and how the different alternatives, which in this case are the consortia that bid for the final contract, were rated and ultimately selected. All the relevant information for this exercise is extracted from the ToR, each consortium's proposal and the final selection process led by INCO. Here, the TETRA preference measurement software will be used to model this multi-criteria selection process and compare the outcomes with the real awarding events. The focus will be only on Tranche 1 (Villeta – The Koran, 78 kilometres).

Note: In order to adequately experiment with the TETRA software, additional bidders were included in the sample (in reality bidders 4 and 5 only bid on tranche 2), and some selection criteria differ slightly from those stated in the ToR. As not all details of the bids were made available, some of the values in Table B.4 are fictitious.

Selection Criteria

The ToR clearly lists and explains the criteria on which INCO would base its selection. Ten different selection criteria form the proposal assessment system. Additionally, each criterion has been assigned a certain weight, which explicitly shows INCO's ranking of interests for this particular project. These ten selection criteria are:

1. Economic proposal.

2. Experience in bridge and viaduct construction.

3. Experience in concession projects for infrastructure.
4. Experience in general construction projects.
5. Experience in road construction.
6. Experience in tunnel construction.
7. Financial capacity.
8. Operative cash flow.
9. Presentation of a project schedule program.
10. Support to the national industry.

Next, a closer look will be taken at each criterion to understand how they would be assessed by INCO.

1. Economic proposal.

   This is the NPV (Net Present Value) associated to the additional contribution that INCO would be responsible to pay to the concessionaire besides the revenues generated from the functioning of toll plazas.

   Economic proposals are assessed according to a price range calculated as follows. First, a reference price is determined by the equation:

$$P = \frac{\bar{X} + M}{2} \tag{B.1}$$

   where P is the price, $\bar{X}$ is the arithmetic mean of the set of economic proposals and M is the median of that set.

   Then, the price range is defined with an upper and a lower limit. The upper limit is defined, thus:

$$Lim_{SUP} = P + 1.5 \times S \tag{B.2}$$

   where S refers to the standard deviation of the set of values of the economic proposals. The lower limit is:

$$Lim_{INF} = 0.8 \times P \tag{B.3}$$

   Within these limits, the economic proposal with the lowest NPV will be awarded eight hundred (800) points. That with the highest, will be awarded zero (0) points; and the rest will get proportionally the corresponding points.

2. Experience in bridge and viaduct construction.

   Each consortium needs to certify its experience in construction of bridges and viaducts. They may certify no more than 5 projects which must be longer than 150 m each. A minimum of 2,000 m of built bridges or viaducts must be ascertained.

   Bids that do not reach these thresholds or that otherwise certify the shortest aggregated built length will get zero (0) points in this selection criterion, while the bid that complies with these two limits and certifies the longest aggregated built length among all the proposals will be awarded two hundred (200) points. The other alternatives will be rated proportionally.

3. Experience in concession projects for infrastructure.

   Each consortium needs to certify that it has participated in at least two concession projects for infrastructure whose financing value was at least US$ 200 million each, or at least one concession project of infrastructure whose financing value was at least US$ 300 million. Here, the term concession project of infrastructure refers to any private or public-private contract carried out as a BDOMFT (Build – Design – Operate – Maintain – Finance – Transfer) contract for infrastructure.

   Bidders that can certify such experience will be granted two hundred (200) points whereas those without will get zero (0) points for this selection criterion. No intermediate scores will be granted.

4. Experience in general construction projects.

   Each bidder is required to demonstrate its experience in construction projects during the last 15 years. At most, 4 infrastructure projects – defined in the ToR as the financing, construction and operation of infrastructure projects in the sectors of energy, drinking water, sewage systems, roads, ports, airports, massive transport systems of passengers, transport of gas, and transport of hydrocarbons – may be presented for this purpose. Those four infrastructure projects' prices must amount to at least US$ 600 million and at least one of them must be more than US$ 300 million.

   Bids that do not reach these thresholds or demonstrate the lowest aggregated value will get zero (0) points in this selection criterion, while the bid that complies with these two limits and demonstrates the highest aggregated price will be awarded two hundred (200) points. The other alternatives will be rated proportionally.

5. Experience in road construction.

   Similarly to criterion 4, each bidder needs to demonstrate its experience in the construction of two-double-lane-corridor roads during the last 15 years. A maximum of three contracts can be certified. They must amount to at least US$ 600 million and at least one of them ought to be worth US$ 300 million or more.

   Bids that do not reach these thresholds will get zero (0) points on this selection criterion, while the bid that complies with these two limits and demonstrates the highest aggregated price will be awarded two hundred (200) points. The other alternatives will be rated proportionally.

6. Experience in tunnel construction.

   Every consortium needs to certify its experience in construction of tunnels. They may be road tunnels or rail tunnels. A maximum of 4 tunnels can be accredited and one of them has to have been at least 2 km long.

   Bids that do not reach these thresholds or that have the shortest tunnel length accredited will get zero (0) points in this selection criterion, while the bid that complies with these two limits and demonstrates that it has built the longest tunnel among all the proposals will be awarded two hundred (200) points. The other alternatives will be rated proportionally.

7. Financial capacity.

   According to each bidder's accounting and financial status as of December 31 2008, balance sheets must certify a minimum equity of US$ 250 million.

   Bidders that do not reach this threshold will get zero (0) points, while those who do will get three hundred (300) points for this selection criterion. No intermediate scores will be granted.

8. Operative cash flow.

   According to each bidder's accounting and financial status as of December 31 2008, balance sheets must certify a minimum operative cash flow of US$ 50 million.

   Bidders that do not reach this threshold will get zero (0) points, while those who do will get three hundred (300) points for this selection criterion. No intermediate scores will be granted.

9. Presentation of a project schedule program.

   Specifying the project's schedule program, through a Gantt chart, that will make part of the final contract and where measurable milestones are clearly identified.

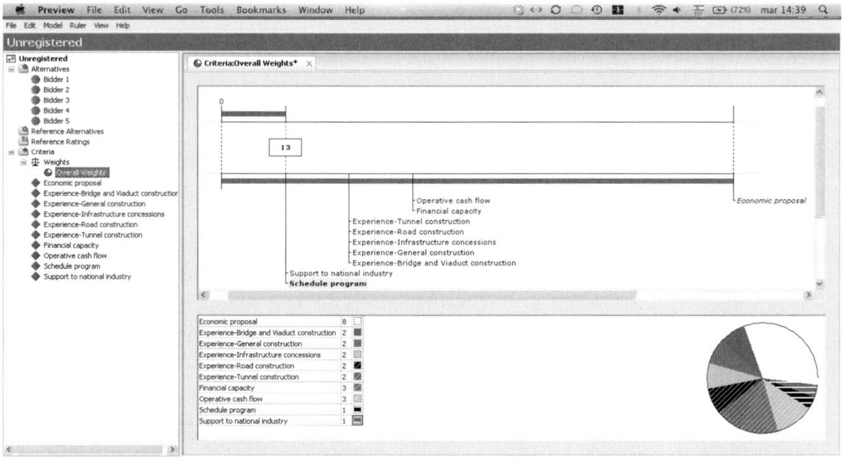

Figure B.3 The weights of the criteria used in the TETRA software.

Those bids that include such a schedule program will be awarded one hundred (100) points. Those that do not include such a schedule program will be awarded zero (0) points. No intermediate scores will be granted.

10. Support to the national industry.

    Seeking to foster the development of national industries, INCO includes this criterion which is meant to award one hundred (100) points to those bidders who are 100% Colombians. Bidders whose shares represent 50% up to 99% of Colombian participation will get fifty (50) points. Finally, proposals with 0% up to 49% of Colombian participation will be awarded zero (0) points.

Since TETRA works with relative weights for each criterion, a criterion was selected as the standard. For this simulation criterion 10 is used. The rest of criteria are weighted proportionally, Figure B.3 shows this relative importance of each criterion.

The bidders

As mentioned earlier, for the preference measurement only the first tranche is taken into account. The five consortia that bid for this tranche are used as alternatives for the TETRA program. Table B.3 lists the five consortia and the partners in each.

Table B.3 The five bidders for the first tranche, and the respective shares of their partners.

Bidder/ Shares	Consortium/ Partner
Bidder 1	Consorcio Vial Helios
30%	Carlos Alberto Solarte (Colombia)
25%	Conconcreto SA (Colombia)
15%	IECSA SA (Argentina)
30%	CSS Builders SA (Colombia)
Bidder 2	Vias del Sol Highway SA Promise of Future Society
15%	Obrascon Huarte Lain SA (Spain)
25%	CONCAY SA (Colombia)
20%	Pavimentos de Colombia SA (Colombia)
25%	Aguilar Construcciones SA (Colombia)
15%	ICEIN (Colombia)
Bidder 3	Highway Development Consortium Ruta del Sol
15%	Mario Huertas Cotes (Colombia)
25%	Constructora OAS Ltda (Brazil)
30%	Procopal SA (Colombia)
15%	Routes Engineering SA (Colombia)
15%	Meyan SA (Colombia)
Bidder 4	Promise of Future Society Plural Structure Concessionary Ruta del Sol
15%	Constructora Norberto Odebrecht (Brazil)
30%	Odebrecht Investimentos em Infra-structure (Brazil)
25%	CSS Builders SA (Brazil)
30%	Estudios y Proyectos del Sol SA - EPISOL (Colombia)
Bidder 5	Temporary concession union "RDS"
20%	MNV S.A. (Colombia); Gas Kapital GR SA
25%	China Railway Shisiju Group Corporation (China)
15%	Great Ways Investment and Engineering Ltd (Colombia)
40%	Inversiones Grandes Vías e Ingeniería Ltda (Colombia)

Bidders' final proposals

This section discusses each bidder's proposal based on the ten criteria. First the real proposed values are presented in Table B.4, and then the data for TETRA ratings is visualized in Figures B.4 to B.13. Because the software needs to have a 0-alternative and a 100-alternative, the alternative with the lowest value has been used as the 0-alternative and the alternative with the highest value has been used as the 100-alternative. Some notes on specific criteria:

- Criterion 7: Financial capacity

  This criterion has only two possible ratings, 0 and 100. Those who have a financial capacity of more than US$ 250 million will receive the maximum and those with less will receive the minimum.

Table B.4 The values of the bidders for criteria 1 to 10.

Bidder	Criterion									
	1 (Mln. US$)	2 (m)	3 (Mln. US$)	4 (Mln. US$)	5 (Mln. US$)	6 (km)	7 (US$)	8 (Mln. US$)	9	10 (%)
Bidder 1	826	272	360	850	1020	2.3	360	120	Y	85
Bidder 2	965	310	257	650	760	3.4	265	40	Y	85
Bidder 3	878	160	465	700	890	1.8	185	150	N	75
Bidder 4	798	320	220	780	580	5.6	230	60	Y	30
Bidder 5	935	120	340	575	930	2.8	170	45	N	75

- Criterion 8: Operative cash flow

  This criterion has only two possible ratings, 0 and 100. Those who have an operative cash flow of more than US$ 50 million will receive the maximum and those with less will receive the minimum.

- Criterion 10: Support to the national industry

  Since none of the bidders was 100% Colombian, a reference alternative was created. This alternative can be seen in Figure B.13, with the label '100% Colombian'.

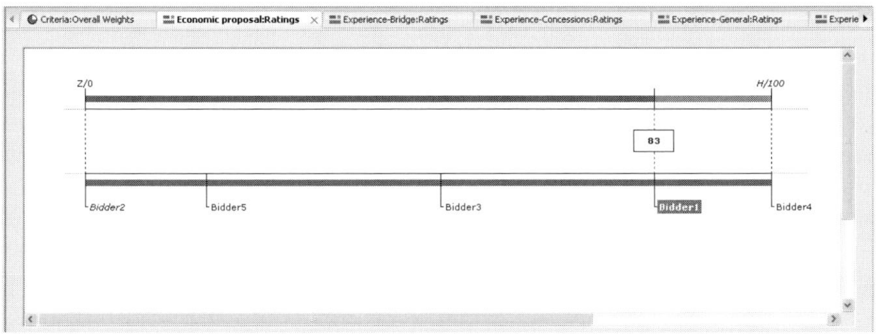

Figure B.4 Scaling the alternatives – criterion 1.

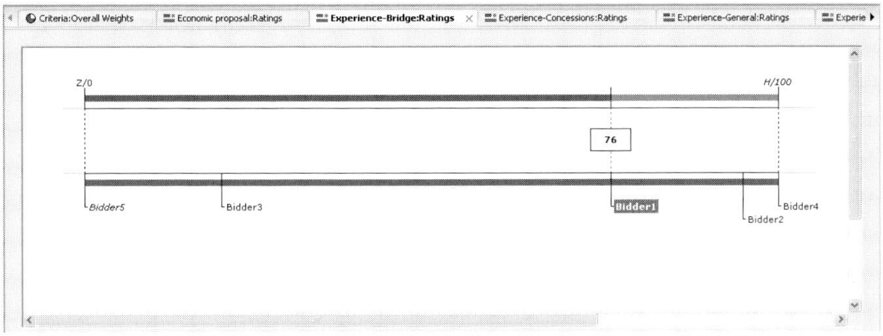

Figure B.5 Scaling the alternatives – criterion 2.

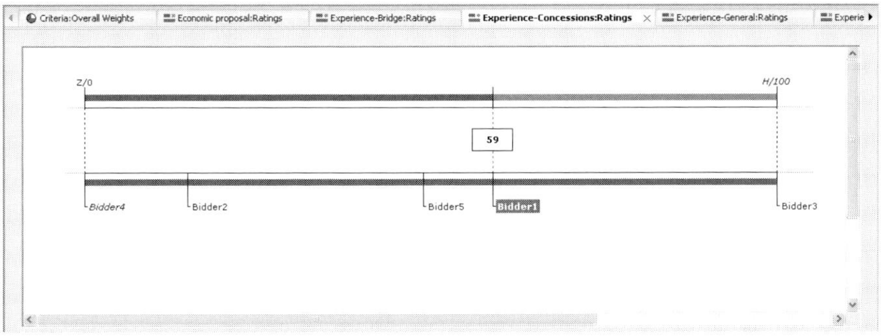

Figure B.6 Scaling the alternatives – criterion 3.

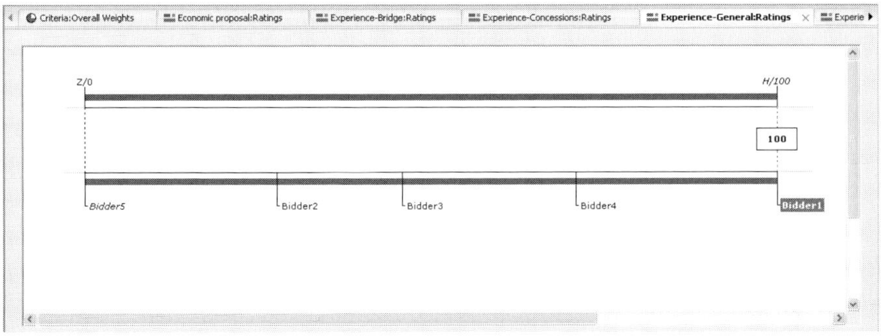

Figure B.7 Scaling the alternatives – criterion 4.

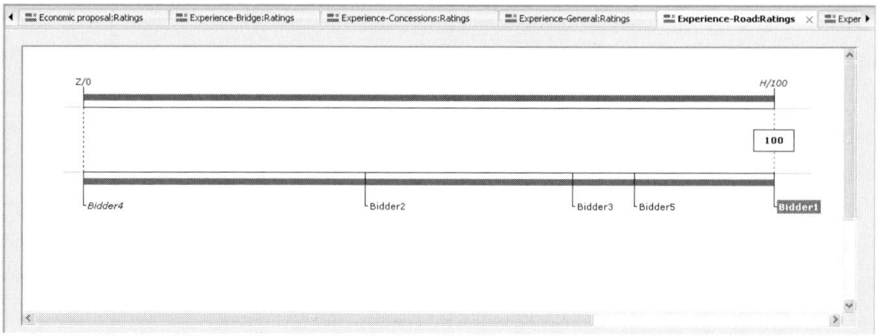

Figure B.8 Scaling the alternatives – criterion 5.

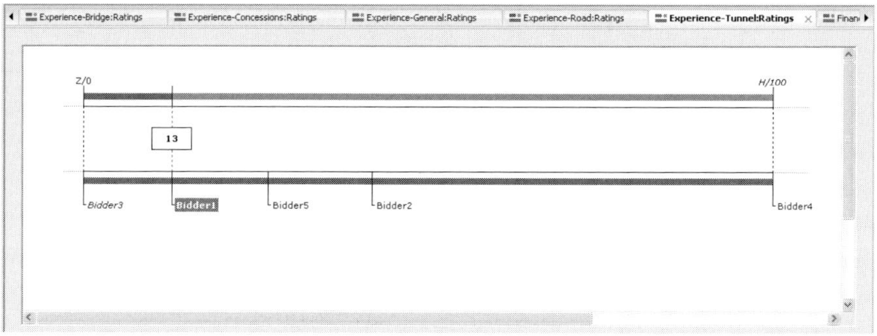

Figure B.9 Scaling the alternatives – criterion 6.

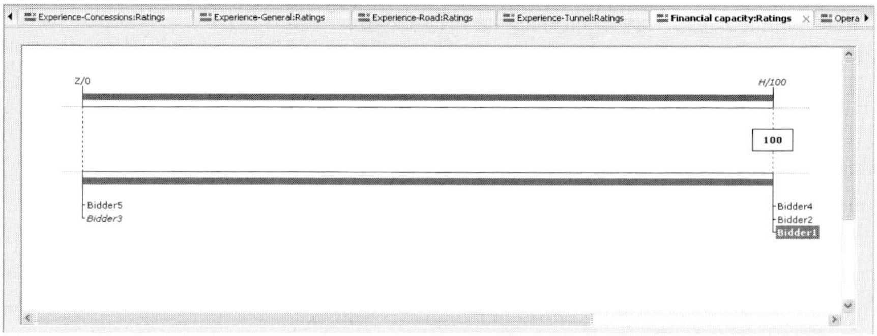

Figure B.10 Scaling the alternatives – criterion 7.

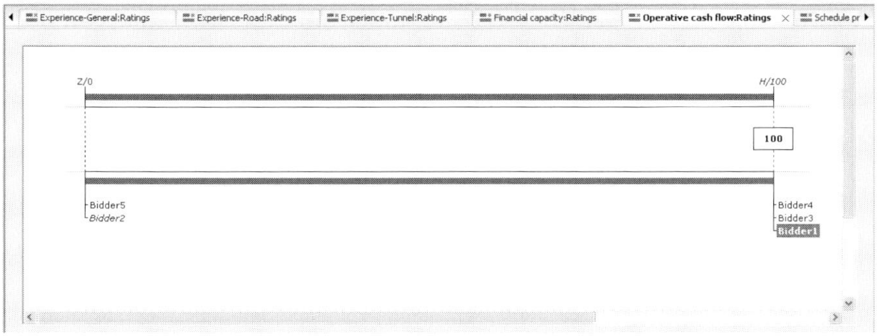

Figure B.11 Scaling the alternatives – criterion 8.

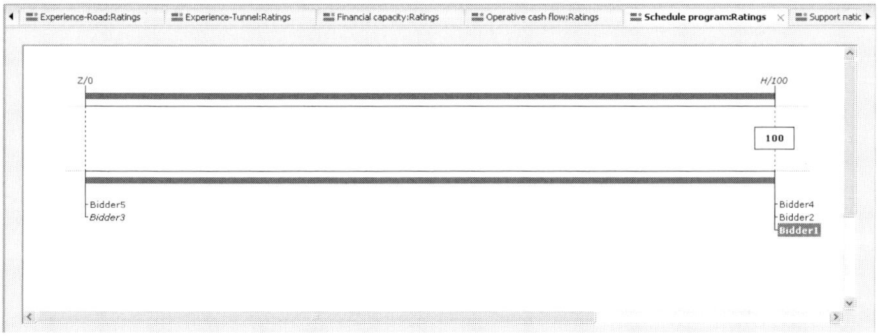

Figure B.12 Scaling the alternatives – criterion 9.

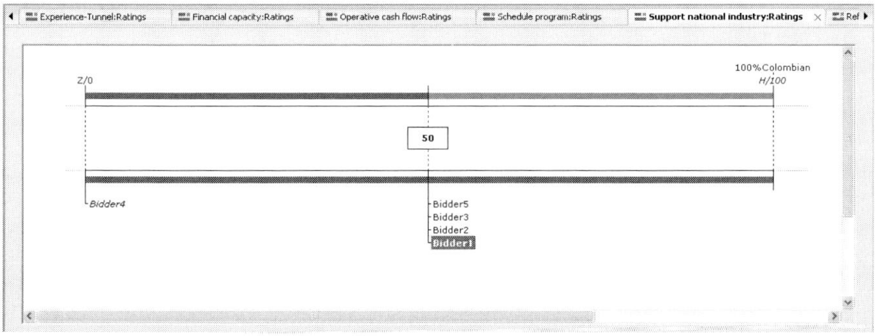

Figure B.13 Scaling the alternatives – criterion 10.

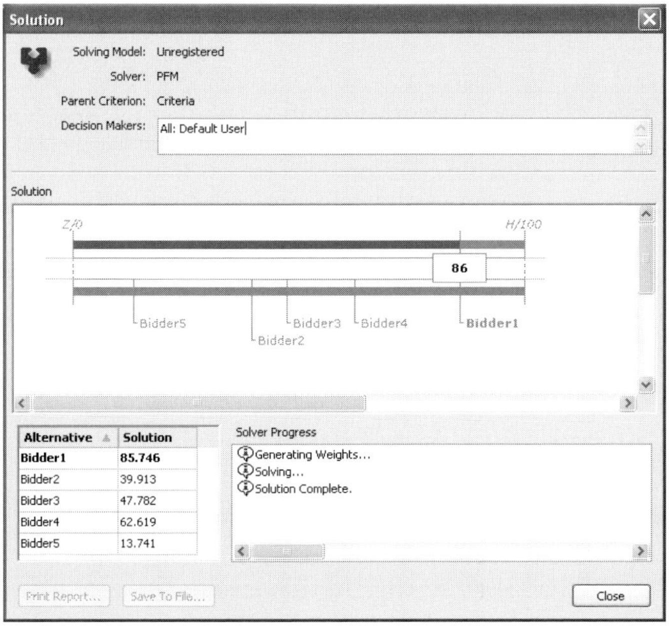

Figure B.14 Outcome of the TETRA software.

Outcome/Conclusion

For this tranche of the project, five consortia made a bid. These five bidders are assessed based on the ten criteria. Every criterion is given a weight and the alternatives are rated. With these two data, the program determines which alternative is the best choice (see Figure B.14).

According to the outcome, bidder 1 (Consorcio Vial Helios) won the awarding. Bidder 1 scored 86 points out the maximum of 100. The second best choice is bidder 4 (Promise of Future Society Plural Structure Concessionary Ruta del Sol) with 63 points.

By assessing the weight of the criteria, some conclusions can be made. First, the focus is on the economic proposal. INCO states that the contribution of INCO should be as low as possible and they see this as very important. The second highest weight was on the operative cash flow and the financial capacity, with a weight of three. This can be seen as a PI management style, which has been discussed in Section B.2.

B.4 Project network planning and mitigation strategy

In the previous section the focus was on the first tranche of the project, the 78 km new road. For the network planning and the mitigation strategy the focus will be on the two tunnels in this tranche. In the whole first tranche there will be three tunnels, with a total length of 3.5 km. Between Villeta and Guaduas are two tunnels, one with a length of 2.2 km (T1) and the other of 1.0 km (T2). Figure B.15 shows the location of the tunnels. Figure B.16 shows the mountainous landscape which has to be dealt with. First a lot of landfill is needed to level the ground. The tunnels will have a width of 12 meters and a height of 7.4 meters. The cross section is visualized in Figure B.17.

The chapter will start with explaining the activities used for the tunnels. For each activity the optimistic, most likely, and pessimistic durations are determined based on experts' estimates. For making the mitigation plan the linkages between the activities are needed, this is done by making a network planning diagram. The next thing to do is testing the mitigation plan, this is done with the MSP (Mitigation Scheduling Program) software. This tool enables the project manager to design mitigation strategies for keeping the project on track. It helps the project manager to react to the unexpected variations the project suffers, which deviate it from the initial schedule. This will lead to a renewed planning including the extra costs and time to be invested.

Note: As these were not available, a fictitious set of mitigations was used. The tunnel construction activities, though, were taken from the original contract between INCO and Consorcio Vial Helios.

Activities

16 main activities are needed to construct the tunnels. In Table B.5 each activity is described and the three estimated durations are mentioned. Because the second tunnel has half the length of the first tunnel, its activity durations are expected to be half that of the first tunnel. They are placed within the brackets. Most of the precedence relations between activities are considered Finish-to-Start relations. Only the precedence relations between *Tunnel excavation* and *Excavation material removal* are modeled as Start-to-Start relation with a lag of 14 days, since those two activities are to be performed simultaneously.

Network planning diagram

To make an overview of the precedence relations between the activities, a network planning diagram is made. This diagram shows the relations between the activities and this figure can be used to determine the critical path. Determining the critical path is done in the next paragraph. Figure B.18 shows the network planning diagram.

Figure B.15 The location of the two tunnels in tranche 1.

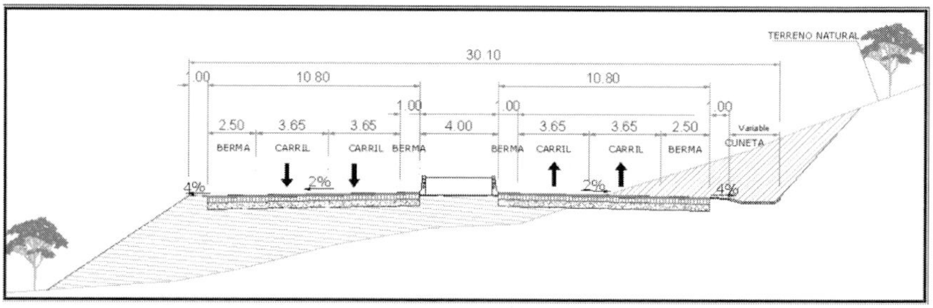

Figure B.16 A cross section of the new road in tranche 1.

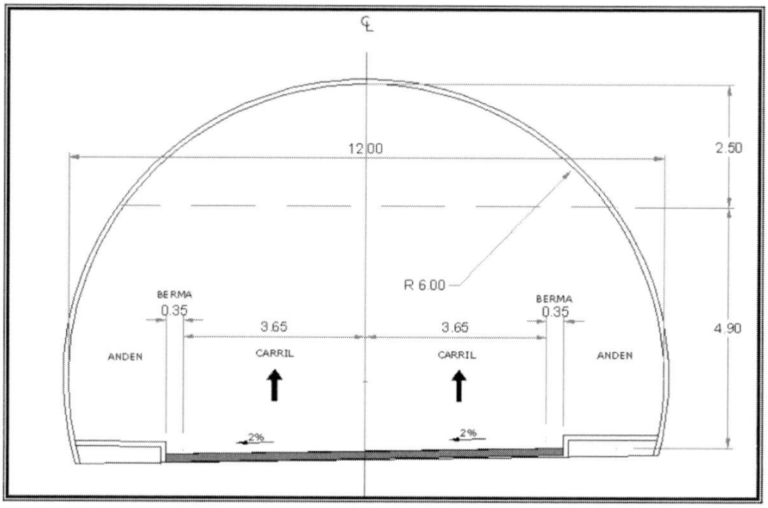

Figure B.17 A cross section of the tunnel in tranche 1.

Table B.5 The 16 main activities.

Activities /	Optimistic duration	Most-likely duration	Pessimistic duration
Initial surveys (01)			
	21 days (11)	28 days (14)	42 days (21)
Before the drawing and calculating can start, first some initial surveys need to be conducted. Surveys need to be conducted are benchmarking and plan metric coordinated data.			
Sample drills (02)			
	21 days (11)	28 days (14)	42 days (21)
By making sample drill, the substance in the soil is determined. This is important to know the strength of the soil.			
Preparation works (03)			
	42 days (21)	56 days (28)	84 days (42)
After the surveys have been conducted, the first preparations are needed. The area has to be leveled out in order to create a good working place.			
Asphalt pavement (04)			
	21 days (11)	28 days (14)	42 days (21)
As mentioned in the introduction of this chapter, this tranche of the project is a new build road. Before the tunnel has started it is possible to create the road on both sides of the tunnel by the pavement of the asphalt.			
Tunnel excavation (05)			
	455 days (228)	504 days (252)	602 days (301)
The tunnels are excavated with a two boom excavating Jumbo. As the name says, it has two arms (booms). First it drills a hole, then it will inject TNT and the ground will come loose.			
Excavation material removal (06)			
	455 days (228)	504 days (252)	602 days (301)
This is needed to clear the tunnel of the rocks and other material after the explosion. For this a Start-to-Start relation with the excavation itself is used. A lag of 14 days is implemented.			
Anchors (07)			
	266 days (133)	336 days (168)	476 days (238)
To make sure that the ceiling will not come done, anchors are used to brace the ceiling. These anchors are also used for placing the steel grid.			
Steel grid (08)			
	280 days (140)	336 days (168)	448 days (224)
The steel grid is used for the reinforcement of the walls and ceilings.			
Sprayed concrete (09)			
	168 days (84)	196 days (98)	252 days (126)
When the steel grid is placed, the concrete will be sprayed on the walls and ceiling.			
Installations (10)			
	98 days (49)	112 days (56)	140 days (70)
To make the tunnel save, some installations are needed. E.g. air fans, lighting and fire protection.			

Continued on the next page...

Activities /	Optimistic duration	Most-likely duration	Pessimistic duration
Concrete pavement (11)			
	42 days (21)	56 days (28)	84 days (42)
To create a flat and robust floor, there will be concrete poured on the floor.			
Steel frames TH-21 (12)			
	119 days (60)	140 days (70)	182 days (91)
The steel frames are used to support the walls and ceiling, they are placed every 4 meters.			
Steel frames TH-36 (13)			
	126 days (63)	140 days (70)	168 days (84)
These frames are used to support the TH-21 steel frames and are placed every 8 meters.			
Drainage (14)			
	42 days (21)	56 days (28)	84 days (42)
Because the area is very mountainous, a good drainage system is required.			
Landfills (15)			
	133 days (67)	168 days (85)	238 days (119)
The land filling is needed for leveling the area.			
Road signalling (16)			
	21 days (11)	28 days (14)	42 days (21)
During this activity the signals, like stripes, are added to the road.			

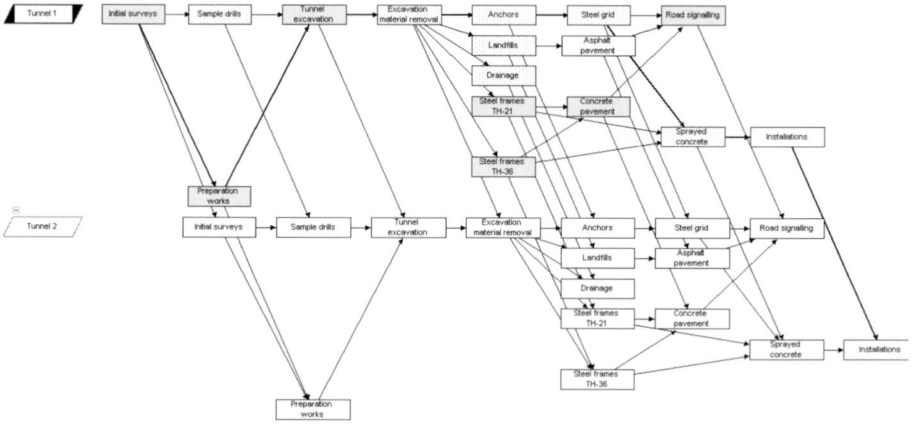

Figure B.18 The network planning diagram.

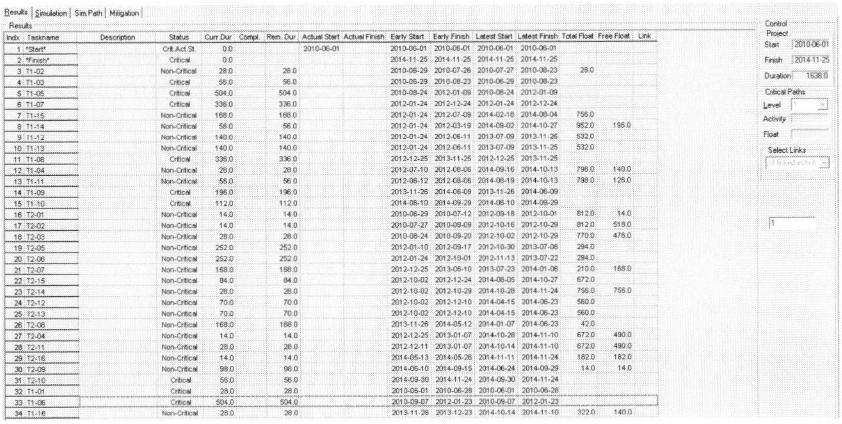

Indx	Taskname	Description	Status	Curr.Dur	Compl.	Rem. Dur	Actual Start	Actual Finish	Early Start	Early Finish	Latest Start	Latest Finish	Total Float	Free Float	Link
1	*Start*		Crit.Act.St.	0.0			2010-06-01		2010-06-01	2010-06-01	2010-06-01	2010-06-01			
2	*Finish*		Critical	0.0					2014-11-25	2014-11-25	2014-11-25	2014-11-25			
3	T1-02		Non-Critical	28.0		28.0			2010-06-29	2010-07-26	2010-07-27	2010-08-23	28.0		
4	T1-03		Critical	56.0		56.0			2010-06-29	2010-08-23	2010-06-29	2010-08-23			
5	T1-05		Critical	504.0		504.0			2010-08-24	2012-01-09	2010-08-24	2012-01-09			
6	T1-07		Critical	336.0		336.0			2012-01-24	2012-12-24	2012-01-24	2012-12-24			
7	T1-15		Non-Critical	168.0		168.0			2012-01-24	2012-07-09	2014-02-18	2014-08-04	756.0		
8	T1-14		Non-Critical	56.0		56.0			2012-01-24	2012-03-19	2014-09-02	2014-10-27	952.0	196.0	
9	T1-12		Non-Critical	140.0		140.0			2012-01-24	2012-06-11	2013-07-09	2013-11-26	532.0		
10	T1-13		Non-Critical	140.0		140.0			2012-01-24	2012-06-11	2013-07-09	2013-11-25	532.0		
11	T1-08		Critical	336.0		336.0			2012-12-25	2013-11-25	2012-12-25	2013-11-25			
12	T1-04		Non-Critical	28.0		28.0			2012-07-10	2012-08-06	2014-09-16	2014-10-13	798.0	140.0	
13	T1-11		Non-Critical	56.0		56.0			2012-06-12	2012-08-06	2014-08-19	2014-10-13	798.0	126.0	
14	T1-09		Critical	196.0		196.0			2013-11-26	2014-06-09	2013-11-26	2014-06-09			
15	T1-10		Critical	112.0		112.0			2014-06-10	2014-09-29	2014-06-10	2014-09-29			
16	T2-01		Non-Critical	14.0		14.0			2010-06-29	2010-07-12	2012-09-18	2012-10-01	812.0	14.0	
17	T2-02		Non-Critical	14.0		14.0			2010-07-27	2010-08-09	2012-10-16	2012-10-29	812.0	518.0	
18	T2-03		Non-Critical	28.0		28.0			2010-08-24	2010-09-20	2012-10-02	2012-10-29	770.0	476.0	
19	T2-05		Non-Critical	252.0		252.0			2012-01-10	2012-09-17	2012-10-30	2013-07-08	294.0		
20	T2-06		Non-Critical	252.0		252.0			2012-01-24	2012-10-01	2012-11-13	2013-07-22	294.0		
21	T2-07		Non-Critical	168.0		168.0			2012-12-25	2013-06-10	2013-07-23	2014-01-06	210.0	168.0	
22	T2-15		Non-Critical	84.0		84.0			2012-10-02	2012-12-24	2014-08-05	2014-10-27	672.0		
23	T2-14		Non-Critical	28.0		28.0			2012-10-02	2012-10-29	2014-10-28	2014-11-24	756.0	756.0	
24	T2-12		Non-Critical	70.0		70.0			2012-10-02	2012-12-10	2014-04-15	2014-06-23	560.0		
25	T2-13		Non-Critical	70.0		70.0			2012-10-02	2012-12-10	2014-04-15	2014-06-23	560.0		
26	T2-08		Non-Critical	168.0		168.0			2013-11-26	2014-05-12	2014-01-07	2014-06-23	42.0		
27	T2-04		Non-Critical	14.0		14.0			2012-12-25	2013-01-07	2014-10-28	2014-11-10	672.0	490.0	
28	T2-11		Non-Critical	28.0		28.0			2012-12-11	2013-01-07	2014-10-14	2014-11-10	672.0	490.0	
29	T2-16		Non-Critical	14.0		14.0			2014-05-13	2014-05-26	2014-11-11	2014-11-24	182.0	182.0	
30	T2-09		Non-Critical	98.0		98.0			2014-06-10	2014-09-15	2014-06-24	2014-09-29	14.0	14.0	
31	T2-10		Critical	56.0		56.0			2014-09-30	2014-11-24	2014-09-30	2014-11-24			
32	T1-01		Critical	28.0		28.0			2010-06-01	2010-06-28	2010-06-01	2010-06-28			
33	T1-06		Critical	504.0		504.0			2010-09-07	2012-01-23	2010-09-07	2012-01-23			
34	T1-16		Non-Critical	28.0		28.0			2013-11-26	2013-12-23	2014-10-14	2014-11-10	322.0	140.0	

Figure B.19 The determining path and expected duration without mitigations.

Table B.6 Critical activities before mitigations.

T1-01	Initial surveys (Tunnel 1)
T1-03	Preparations works (Tunnel 1)
T1-05	Tunnel excavation (Tunnel 1)
T1-06	Excavation material removal (Tunnel 1)
T1-07	Anchors (Tunnel 1)
T1-08	Steel grid (Tunnel 1)
T1-09	Sprayed concrete (Tunnel 1)
T1-10	Installations (Tunnel 1)
T2-10	Installations (Tunnel 2)

MSP results without mitigations

The information discussed in the previous sections is used in the MSP software. This led to the following figures and conclusions.

Figure B.19 shows the basic results obtained from the MSP software where the expected start and finish dates and expected project duration are calculated and where the critical activities that compose the critical path are identified. Hereby, the expected project duration resulted in 1,638 days and the expected critical path is made of the activities listed in Table B.6.

After performing a Monte Carlo simulation 5,000 times with the MSP software, a frequency distribution of the possible project durations is obtained, based on the three estimates assigned previously to each activity. This probability distribution resulted from a network planning with no mitigation plans. Figure B.20 shows the probability of the different project durations. For example, the project has a probability of 60% to be completed within 1769 days and the project is certainly finished within 2623 days. MSP also determines the mean of the probabilities, for this project the mean is 1751 days. The most interesting outcome though, is the low probability of finishing the project within the 1,638 days initially expected. There is only a probability of almost 20% of complying with this expected duration.

Figure B.21 explains the cumulative distribution of the outcome. It basically visualizes the same as the previous figure, but it is easier to read and the exact probability of the initially expected duration can be spotted.

As mentioned above, MSP is also able to determine the critical path, this is best visualized in the following Gantt chart. The yellow bar is an activity which is on the critical path. Green bars are non-critical activities, these activities deserve less attention during the project since they do not affect the project duration, for they have a degree of float. However, after running the Monte Carlo simulation, MSP not only determines one most probable critical path, but also secondary critical paths with lower probabilities. These secondary critical paths can become the first critical path during the project. Hence, it is wise to consider not just one critical path when designing or adopting mitigation strategies, but also less probable critical paths. Figure B.22 depicts the Gantt chart determined by MSP software before applying mitigations.

After running the simulations with MSP, several critical paths with their respective probabilities are calculated. This enables the project manager to plan mitigation measures not only for the activities on the first critical path but also on the less probable critical activities. Figure B.23 shows that some T1 activities are consistently on the critical path. These activities deserve utmost attention for the implementation of mitigating measures. This information is useful for designing mitigation strategies for specific tasks. Table B.7 shows the probability that an activity falls within a critical path. From this table, the project manager may decide which activities to mitigate based on the probabilities of them falling within a critical path.

Possible mitigations

Thus, the following mitigation strategies were considered. Their respective costs and implications are hereby explained. The numbers are based on rough calculation of the INCO Terms of References.

- Mitigation 1 (T1-05)

  Description: A second work front for tunnel one. For this, an extra two boom Jumbo is needed and trucks to remove the material.

  Reduced duration: This will lead to a 70 day reduction in excavation and removing the excavated material.

  Extra costs: This mitigation implies an extra cost of US$ 1.5 million

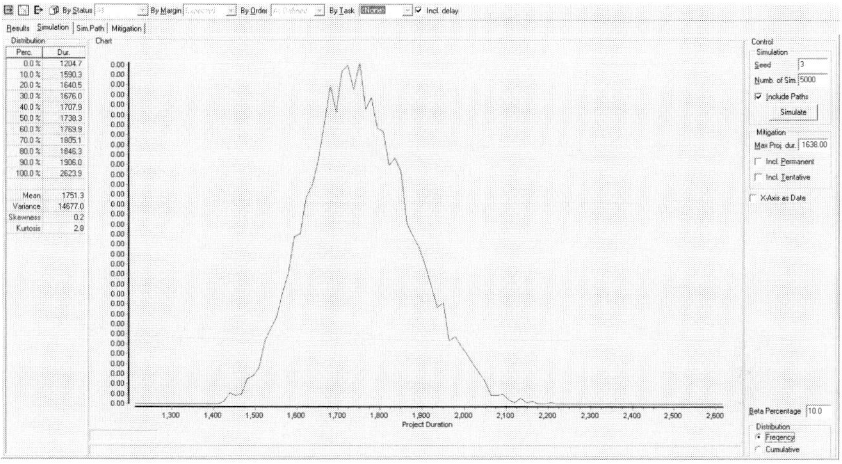

Figure B.20 The frequency distribution of the project duration without mitigations.

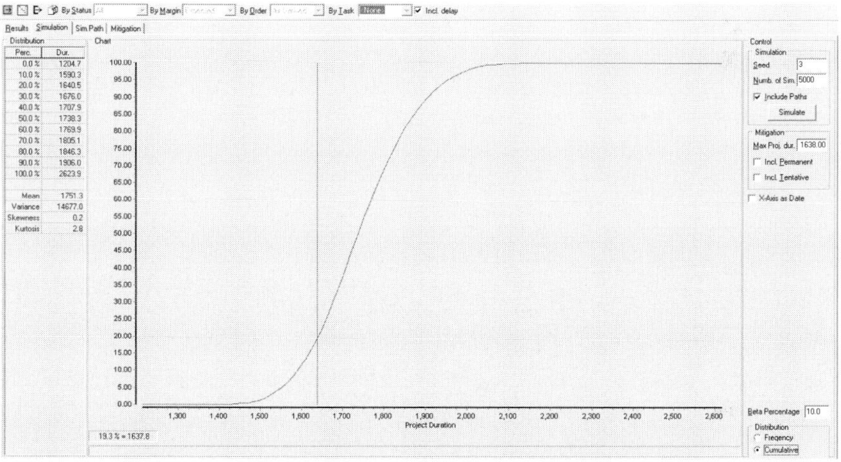

Figure B.21 The cumulative distirbution of the project duration without mitigations.

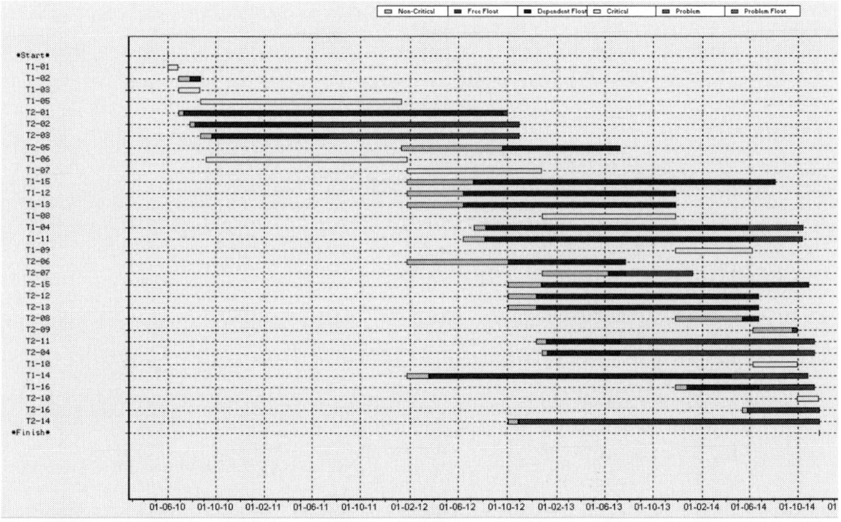

Figure B.22 The Gantt chart without mitigations.

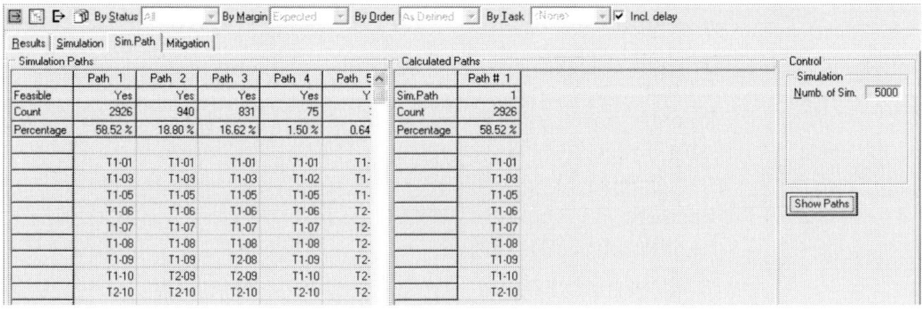

Figure B.23 The critical paths determined by MSP.

Table B.7 The activities and their probability to be on one of the critical path.

Activities		Probability (%)
T1-01	Initial surveys (Tunnel 1)	100.0
T1-02	Sample drills (Tunnel 1)	1.5
T1-03	Preparations works (Tunnel 1)	98.5
T1-04	Asphalt pavement (Tunnel 1)	0.0
T1-05	Tunnel excavation (Tunnel 1)	100.0
T1-06	Excavation material removal (Tunnel 1)	100.0
T1-07	Anchors (Tunnel 1)	100.0
T1-08	Steel grid (Tunnel 1)	100.0
T1-09	Sprayed concrete (Tunnel 1)	84.0
T1-10	Installations (Tunnel 1)	60.0
T1-11	Concrete pavement (Tunnel 1)	0.0
T1-12	Steel frames TH-21 (Tunnel 1)	0.0
T1-13	Steel frames TH-36 (Tunnel 1)	0.0
T1-14	Drainage (Tunnel 1)	0.0
T1-15	Landfills (Tunnel 1)	0.0
T1-16	Road signalling (Tunnel 1)	0.0
T2-01	Initial surveys (Tunnel 2)	0.0
T2-02	Sample drills (Tunnel 2)	0.0
T2-03	Preparations works (Tunnel 2)	0.0
T2-04	Asphalt pavement (Tunnel 2)	0.0
T2-05	Tunnel excavation (Tunnel 2)	0.0
T2-06	Excavation material removal (Tunnel 2)	0.0
T2-07	Anchors (Tunnel 2)	0.0
T2-08	Steel grid (Tunnel 2)	16.5
T2-09	Sprayed concrete (Tunnel 2)	35.0
T2-10	Installations (Tunnel 2)	100.0
T2-11	Concrete pavement (Tunnel 2)	0.0
T2-12	Steel frames TH-21 (Tunnel 2)	0.0
T2-13	Steel frames TH-36 (Tunnel 2)	0.0
T2-14	Drainage (Tunnel 2)	0.0
T2-15	Landfills (Tunnel 2)	0.0
T2-16	Road signalling (Tunnel 2)	0.0

- Mitigation 2 (T1-09)

  Description: Using fast track concrete that reduces the drying time of the concrete. This is only implemented for tunnel one.

  Reduced duration: By using the fast track concrete, the drying time is reduced by 30%, this is 59 days.

  Extra costs: The costs will also be 30%, which is US$ 1.2 million

- Mitigation 3 (T1-10)

  Description: By contracting a second subcontractor for the installations both tunnels can be done at the same time. This will change the relation between the two activities from Finish-to-Start to Start-to-Start. As the software currently does not support a change in relation as a mitigation, the duration of installing the installation in tunnel one is reduced.

  Reduced duration: This will reduce the duration with 56 days.

  Extra costs: This will increase the costs with US$ 1.0 million.

- Mitigation 4 (T1-08)

  Description: The steel grids are place by one group, it is possible to hire more people or more experienced people. If this is done in tunnel one, time can be reduced.

  Reduced duration: By implementing this mitigation, the duration will be reduced by 56 days.

  Extra costs: This will increase the costs with US$ 1.0 million.

- Mitigation 5 (T1-07)

  Description: Placing the anchors is a very specialized activity, when this is done with non-specialized workers it will take longer. By hiring specialized contractors for tunnel one, time can be saved.

  Reduced duration: This can reduce time by 75 days.

  Extra costs: This will increase the costs with US$ 750,000.

MSP results with mitigations

As shown before the probability of finishing within the expected duration (1,638 days) is unacceptably low. That is why a first run with tentative mitigations is performed, resulting in Figure B.24. The program sees mitigation 1 (T1-07) as effective and uses it in almost 52% of the time. It is decided to make this mitigation permanent.

With one permanent mitigation and four tentative mitigations, the program is run a second time to see what the new probability of finishing within time

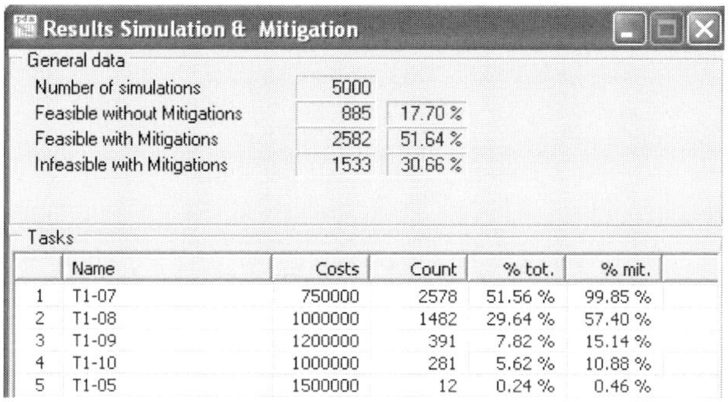

Figure B.24 The results of the first run in MSP.

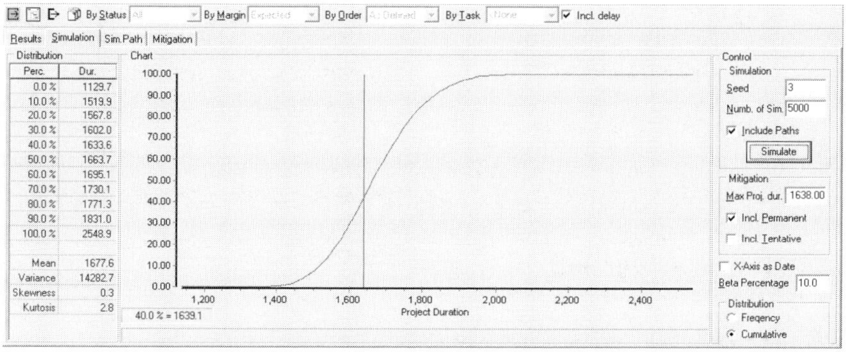

Figure B.25 The cumulative distribution after the first run.

is. This leads to Figure B.25. The probability has increased from 19.3% to 40%, which is still unacceptably low. That is why a second simulation has been performed. This leads to Figure B.26.

T1-08 has been used 29,64% of the time and is therefore also included as permanent mitigation. With these settings, the cumulative distribution in Figure B.27 is determined. The probability has increased to almost 60%, which is considered to be acceptable, taking into account mitigation costs and possible delay penalties.

Finally, the project manager, responsible for finishing the project in time, has to keep in mind that a total of US$ 1.75 million has to be reserved for at least these two mitigations, if he expects to have a fair probability of delivering the project within the agreed time duration.

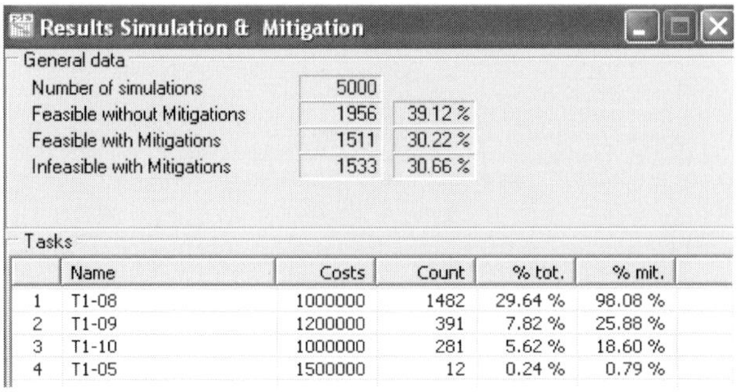

Figure B.26 The results of the second run in MSP.

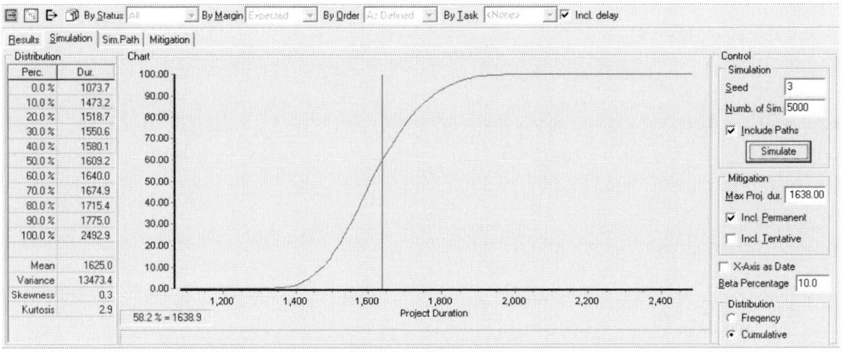

Figure B.27 The cumulative distribution after the second run.

B.5 Conclusions

This case has analyzed the various concepts addressed by the theory of Open Design and Construction Management. First, a close look was given to two different ways of managing construction projects, PI vs. PII management practices. Although it is recommended to address very large and complex projects, characterized by uncertainty and a multiplicity of stakeholders, with PII-like management practices, their subtasks, which may be quite straightforward processes, are better managed with the traditional PI approach. This shows that the two approaches are not exclusive but complementary. The case study analyzed in this document presents both management approaches. Rare as this may be for Colombian standard procedures, INCO managed to make use of PII-like practices and thus has been acknowledged by national and international entities for leading such an important project to the country with clarity and transparency as far as its initial stages are concerned.

Secondly, this case study has been used for comprehending the basics of

Preference Measurement with the help of TETRA software. This software delivered the same results as in the real case study for the selection outcome of the tendering process. It may be concluded that Preference Measurement can only be conducted after a clear definition of a measurement scale and that TETRA is a highly useful software when any decision-making process requires the ranking intervention of several stakeholders. Hence, TETRA could be a potential improving tool, among others, for awarding processes in public and private tenders.

Finally, the Ruta del Sol project has been used as input for implementing a state-of-the-art tool in network planning with on-the-run mitigations. This tool has been shown greatly useful for planning activities of large and complex projects like this one where uncertainty and unexpected events demand timely actions from the project manager. This tool was found to be very helpful for project managers who need to decide upon the best alternatives that shall redirect his or her project onto the right track. MSP software enables the future project manager of Ruta del Sol project to choose the most effective and efficient mitigation strategies that can best suit the rest of the project constraints.

References

Gunsteren, L. A. van (2011), *Stakeholder-oriented Project Management, Tools and Concepts*, IOS Press, Delft.

Instituto Nacional de Concesiones (2008), *Project presentation*, Bogota, Colombia.

Instituto Nacional de Concesiones (2010), *Presentation of the organization*, at: http://www.inco.gov.co/FormsWeb/WF_Default.aspx (accessed 7 March 2010).

Instituto Nacional de Vias, *Mission and Vision of INVIAS*, at: http://www.invias.gov.co/ (accessed 7 March 2010).

International Finance Corporation, *The vision of IFC*, at: http://www.ifc.org/ifcext/about.nsf/Content/Mission (accessed 7 March 2010).

Medella, E., (2010), "Inco plans to award 3rd stretch of Ruta del Sol in June", *Business News Americas*, available at: http://www.bnamericas.com/news/privatization/ Concession_ of_Ruta_del_Sol*s_third_stretch_ to_be_awarded_in_June, (accessed 7 March 2010).

Ministerio de Transporte (2009), *Mission, Vision and Objectives of MdT*, at: http://www.mintransporte.gov.co/Ministerio/presentacion.html (accessed 7 March 2010).

C Case: Nieuw Zaailand

C.1 Introduction to the project

The occasion

Already in 2004 there was an initiative to improve the city centre of Leeuwarden (Figure C.1)[1]. The 'Outline for a Masterplan'[2] stated that Leeuwarden could improve its shopping area by improving the 'Zaailand' region. It has a central position, a parking garage under the square, and a differentiated retail business already existing in the area. There was also the chance to transform Zaailand into the 'living-room' of Leeuwarden, due to the legacy of the architect Abe Bonnema. He dedicated his legacy to the Fries Museum, under the condition that it would be spent on a new building for this Museum, on the Zaailand. This gave the opportunity to combine the 'daily culture' of shopping and going out, with the 'high culture' of a museum.

The project 'Nieuw Zaailand' consists of four parts: the underground parking garage, the retail/dwelling 'strip', the museum, and a shopping centre (Figure C.2). These four different parts are strongly interrelated. The museum stands partly on the parking garage, the retail/dwelling strip continues under the museum, and it all has to be built in this small inner-city area, at the same time. This means the project is complex with a lot of interfaces and a lot of stakeholders.

The Nieuw Zaailand project is now at the point of being realised.

The progress

In 2004 the first step to a Masterplan for Nieuw Zaailand was made. Until the realisation (2009) a lot has happened. A short description of the important developments will be described here.

Decision-making on the strip

Initially the designs of the project were all made by the architect Hubert-Jan Henket. Unfortunately for him there was a large aversion from the population to his design for the retail/dwelling strip. His design is very sober and people did not like that kind of architecture in the city centre. Because of this unrest the council of the municipality felt pressure to do something with this strip. The municipality decided to let new architects, Soeters Van Eldonk, make the design of the strip. Their architecture was much more playful and they work with more colour than Henket.

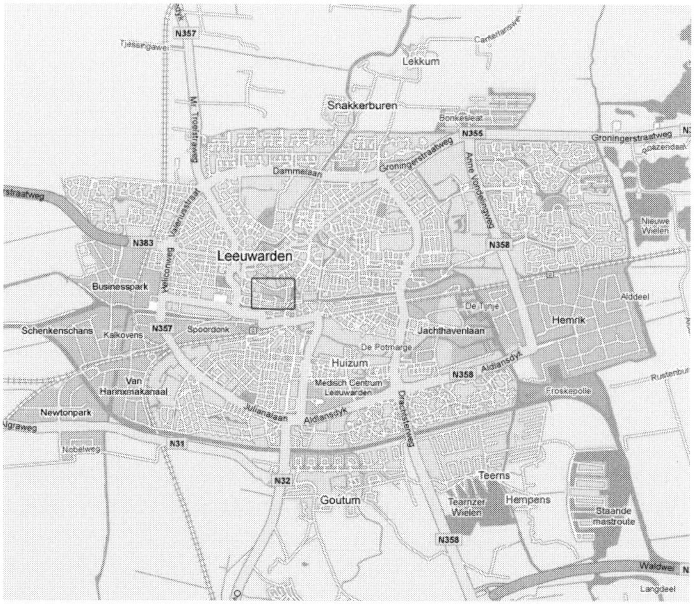

Figure C.1 Area of Nieuw Zaailand.

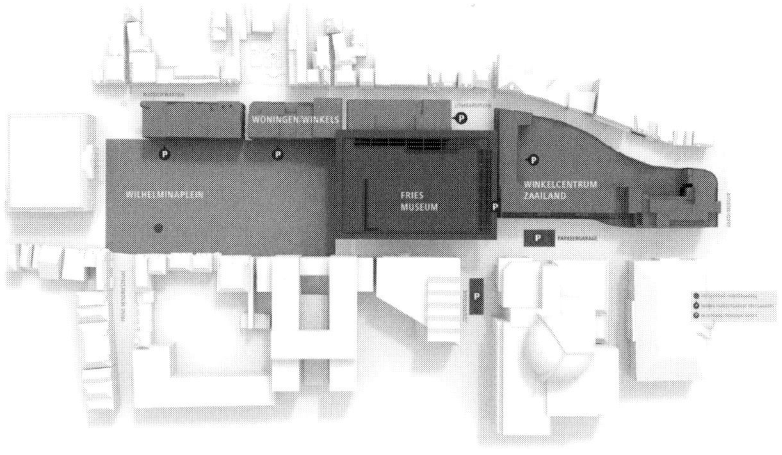

Figure C.2 The four different parts of Nieuw Zaailand.

Besides the problem with the architecture, there was also concern about the impact that this strip could have on the square. People thought the square would become too small or the street behind it too narrow. Apart from these problems, there were a lot of citizens against the project as a whole. People thought it was unnecessary to replace the museum, which had been rebuilt ten years earlier. Also, people were suspicious because the legacy of Bonnema was kept secret.

To overcome this pressure on the project, the municipality decided to introduce a referendum to let the citizens decide on the project. People could vote for or against the project and they could vote for different alternatives (with or without strip). The referendum was not binding for the council, but in the end the attendance of the referendum was also too low to take a decision based on the referendum. The full strip as designed by Soeters Van Eldonk was taken into the final design. Still, the introduction of a referendum had created a large delay on the project.

The decision making on the strip and the whole project will be elaborated in Section C.4.

Cooperation between the clients

At the start of the project, ING Real Estate was the developer of the strip and IPMMC was the delegated developer of the Fries Museum[3]. In a later stadium, IPMMC took over the development of the strip from ING Real Estate. IPMMC also received the project management role for the parking garage, which meant that they had a large part of the project in their own house. The idea of IPMMC was to create synergy and become more efficient because of this bundling of tasks. The shopping centre of Nieuw Zaailand is owned by Syntrus Achmea Vastgoed and will also be developed by this company. The municipality of Leeuwarden is the developer of the public space and Stichting Parkeergarages Leeuwarden of the parking garage.

The project organisation had decided to communicate as one project to the external world, e.g. the public. For the four projects, one communication working group was created. The tendering of the project was divided into two different parts. On one hand there was the shopping centre, which functions independently, and on the other hand the combination of the parking garage, the retail/dwelling strip, the Fries Museum and the public space, which are united in one complete tender.

For the cooperation between the different clients (municipality, IPMMC, Fries Museum, Syntrus Achmea) a 'development agreement' was created, to help the organisation over the course of the project. The development of this agreement has taken a very long time, which had a large impact on the overall duration of the project.

C.2 Management style

PI vs. PII management

In Binnekamp et al. (2006)[4] a comparison is made between PI and PII management using ten aspects. All aspects will be discussed very briefly here (Table C.1). Three aspects notable in this project will be elaborated upon: goal setting, progress control, and integration and coordination of tasks. The progress control will be described in Section C.3. Goal setting and integration and coordination of tasks will be discussed here.

> *Observation on PI vs. PII:* It is important to see that the starting point of PI is the fastest. You pick your goal and you take the shortest way to there. It could happen that people are not happy with your goal or you route and appeal to your plans. In the end this can cause a lot of delays. PII takes more a 'detour', but will most of the time not be confronted with appeals and problems in a later stage of the project, because most of the objections, opinions and stakes are already taken into account.

Goal setting: separation of design and construction

In this project the goal setting was done during the design phase. When this phase was finished the goal was fully set and the construction began. Now a lot of knowledge of the contractor was not used in the design stage. This knowledge could be useful on aspects such as inner city building, planning, sequence of building, etc. When this cooperation is created it could also be used to make sure that the important deadline was attainable. Even within European regulations this is possible with alliance contracts, for example.

Also the selection of the contractor can be done on more aspects than lowest price. This could be used to select the contractor on its experience with inner city work.

Integration and coordination of tasks: development agreement

A lot of time is spent on the 'development agreement': getting all the cooperation rules on paper. Open Design proposes to delegate work on the basis of trust. This could definitely be more efficient. Of course, this is easier said than done. The tricky thing here is that Open Design assumes one organisation, where in this project there are several organisations that have to work together as one client. The theory of Open Design does not give enough help here.

Table C.1 PI vs. PII in project Nieuw Zaailand.

Aspect	PI	PII	Nieuw Zaailand	Good? Different?
Goal Setting	Set goals at start and separate design and construction.	Adjust goals when circumstances change and insight improves.	PI: Separation of design and construction.	See Section C.2.
Leadership	Project manager is central figure in entire process (with a lot of reference power).	Leadership aimed at focusing on relevant stakeholders' interests	PII: Leadership is shared with all relevant stakeholders in 'development agreement'	All stakes are represented, but as can be seen, this can slow down the project.
Conflict resolution	Defined limits of formal and sanction power, power structure determines outcome (powerful stakeholders!)	Equal treatment of powerful and less powerful and of experts and laymen, valid information determines outcome.	PII: The opinion of the citizens (which are generally less powerful stakeholders) was taken into account in the referendum.	The less powerful stakeholders are introduced in the process, but again this slows down the project.
Design process	Focus on solution (point) and freeze design when necessary to keep the deadlines.	Think in solution space; respect 'constraint ownership'[5]: no change without stakeholder consent.	PI to PII: At first the design was fully set, only after a lot of unrest 'more space was created around the solution'.	In this case it was maybe wiser to start with PII and start with solution space.
Communication	Communication is information oriented.	Provide valid information to whoever needs it; decision oriented.	PI: Information is provided to each other and to 'the outside' without knowing whether someone needs that information.	PII would be better here, but the question is whether it is possible to find out what information people need.

Continued on the next page...

Aspect	PI	PII	Nieuw Zaailand	Good? Different?
Persuasion of players	Attention to PR and image building and use of powerful audio-visual aids.	Accept consequences of being honest no matter what.	-	-
Progress control	Small steps with identifiable milestones against planned deadlines.	Pay attention to formal and informal information and anticipate pro-actively.	PI: A planning with milestones is used, no pro-active adjustments on planning.	A suggestion for a PII planning is made in Section C.3.
Division of tasks	Defined in job and function descriptions; responsibility of right information at right place in job description: information push.	Think in roles instead of job descriptions; make groups responsible for information they need: information pull.	-	-
Integration and coordination of tasks	Responsibility of project manager, little reliance on personal initiatives.	Allow project manager to delegate tasks to people he/she trusts.	PI/PII: PI: Coordination is strictly denoted in 'development agreement' (lack of trust?); PII: project is divided into several sub-projects, natural delegation.	The PI-aspect of writing everything on coordination down is not helping the project. Trust should somehow be generated. See Section C.2.
Standardisation	As much as possible, standardisation reduces complexity.	Only where functional and genuinely accepted by stakeholders.	PI to PII: One architect for different parts could be a form of standard-isation. Again, because of unrest, 'a switch to PII' was made.	If the opinion of the citizens was known from the beginning, the switch of architects would not have been made.

Conclusions

Table C.1 shows us that in this project PI as well as PII management styles are used. Both have their advantages.

It is clear that PI management (clear goal setting, involving not too many people, using power to reach decisions, etc.) can be an effective way of management. This style has a lot of speed and projects can be realised sooner. Unfortunately, this management style leads more often to appeals or problems with changing goals, which in the end lead to delays. This means it is not always an efficient way of management.

PII management (involving those that have an interest, being honest and open, working with solution spaces, etc.) is a way of project management that could be more efficient, because all stakes are involved and no power games are played. This needs a lot of investment in the beginning of the project (time and money) that some people think they do not have.

It is hard to find a balance in this trade-off between getting to your goal as fast as possible and investing in the beginning of the project in the right goal. A project manager should always consider both management styles.

Cooperation between parties should be built on trust rather than on contracts and rules. A lot of time is spent (lost) on the 'development agreement', getting all the cooperation rules on paper, while it might be more efficient to build on trust. Of course, this is easier said than done. The theory of Open Design does not give enough help here.

A lot of knowledge is lost when design and realisation are separated. There could be gain in involving a contractor in the design phase, because of the difficult inner city problems and the strict deadline. European regulations should not be boundary for this.

C.3 Planning

Planning as used

For this report the planning is used that was dated 23rd of May 2007, as shown in Figure C.3. At the moment of writing, a delay of nine months has occurred (difference in planning of the start of the realisation). This delay is mostly created by delays in cooperation agreements between the clients and the delay in the design phase, partly created by the referendum.

Planning in Open Design

To implement the used planning in the MSP software[6] additional information is needed. This is largely based on information supplied by Arthur Suiker[7].

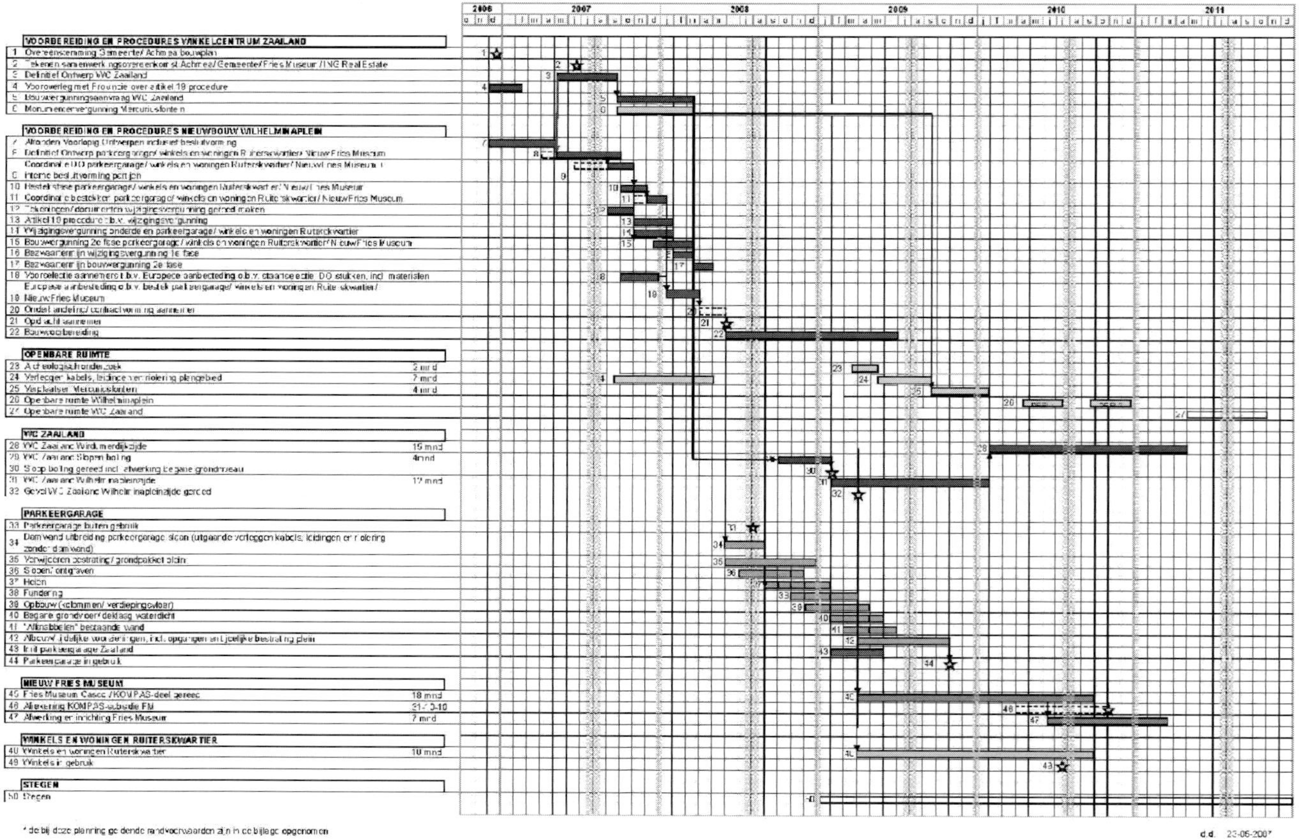

Figure C.3 Overall planning Nieuw Zaailand (d.d. 23 May 2007).

First of all, a probabilistic distribution has to be added to the tasks. The following assumption was made to do this.

Assumption: The tasks were divided into three groups: short (less than 12 weeks), medium (12 to 24 weeks), and long (more than 24 weeks). The optimistic planning is minus 1, 2, 4 weeks respectively and the pessimistic planning is plus 2, 4, 8 weeks respectively.

A few exceptions are made on this assumption. These are:

- Task 4: maximum duration 52 weeks;
- Task 5: uncertainty doubled;
- Task 17: maximum duration 52 weeks;
- Task 19: maximum duration +4 weeks (=14 weeks);
- Task 20: maximum duration +3 weeks (=11 weeks);
- Task 23: maximum duration 52 weeks;
- Task 25: smaller uncertainty because of specific plan.

Possibilities for mitigations also needed to be introduced. For the reduction of the duration an assumption has to be made.

Assumption: the reduction of the duration by mitigation is equal to 2 (small), 4 (medium), or 8 (large) weeks.

A few exceptions are made on this assumption. These are:

- Task 3: smaller reduction;
- Task 8-12: smaller reduction (already quite optimised);
- Task 22: double reduction (radical measures);
- Task 33-49: half of the reduction (also half of the costs).

Because the costs of these mitigations are not known and only the ratio between them is important, the following assumption is made.

Assumption: the costs of mitigation are equal to the duration of the task.

In this way, mitigations for large tasks will have high costs and mitigations for small tasks will have low costs. A few exceptions are made on this assumption. These are:

- Task 22: triple costs because of financial risks;

- Task 33-49: half of the costs (also half of the reduction of time).

Milestones are not added to the program, as the software has no possibility for milestones.

With all this information entered, the program will simulate the project 50,000 times. The first time this is done without the mitigations. The result is a distribution function of the probability of the project duration, shown in Figure C.4. A cumulative distribution function is shown in Figure C.5. As can be seen in the figures, the probability of finishing on time[8] is only 0.9%. This is not realistic, because no project manager would let his project run over time that often without doing anything. Therefore mitigations are introduced.

Because the program cannot handle all mitigations at the same time, the first simulation with mitigations is done with only the mitigation of task 7. The result of this simulation (with permanent[9] mitigation) is shown in Figures C.6 and C.7. The probability of finishing on time is now already increased to 24.8%. With adding also mitigation 10, this becomes 37.0% (Figure C.8). After some trying, the best result was achieved with mitigations on task 7, 10, 11 and 47. The probability of finishing on time is then 86,7% (Figure C.9).

The Gantt chart of the planning is shown in Figure C.10. The critical path did not change compared to the situation without mitigations. This means that the mitigations did not have enough impact to change the critical path (this is not necessary). It is evident that the effective mitigations are thus all on the critical path.

Conclusions

The planning as it is used in the project right now is infrequently adjusted to the current situation, by transferring delayed to a later point. At the end of the project one has to find out whether enough of a 'hurry' was made in the first phase of the project to accommodate these remaining delayed tasks.

With this tool one can simulate the project, including the chances that a task takes longer or shorter, and see how often certain mitigations are used to realise the project on time. A project manager then knows which mitigations he can take with certainty and which mitigations are very effective and should be taken into account.

In this project the critical path is very tight and therefore all mitigations that have impact are on the critical path. Nevertheless one should always be aware of the possibility that mitigations can cause a change of the critical path, which means another focus for finishing the project on time.

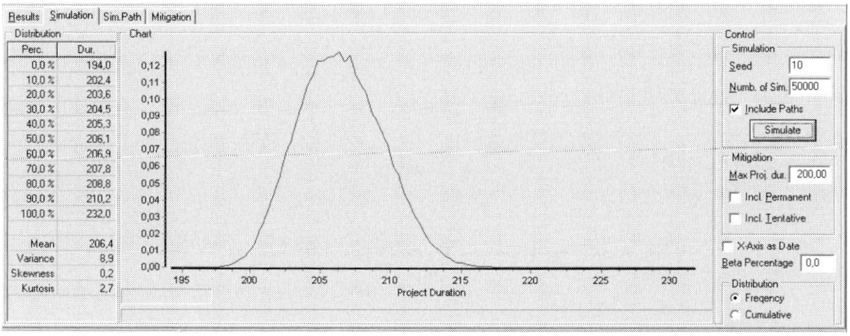

Figure C.4 Probability density function of project duration without mitigations.

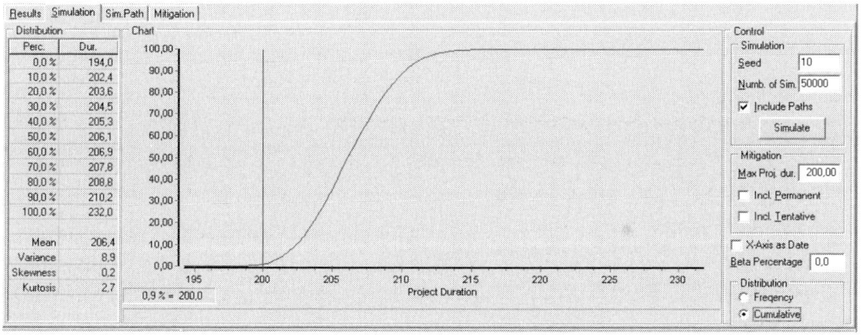

Figure C.5 Cumulative distribution function of project duration without mitigations.

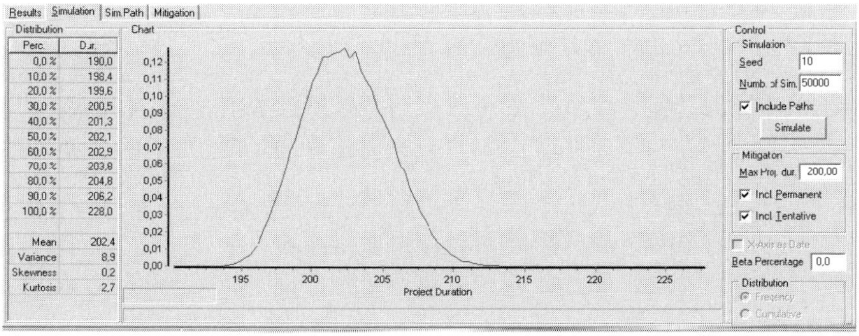

Figure C.6 Probability density function of project duration with mitigation of task 7.

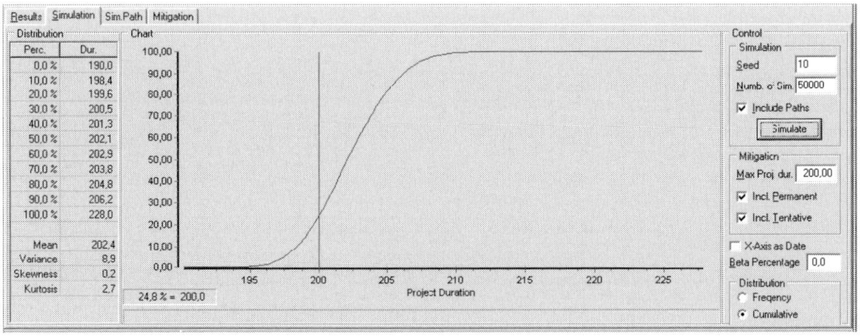

Figure C.7 Cumulative distribution function of project duration with mitigation of task 7.

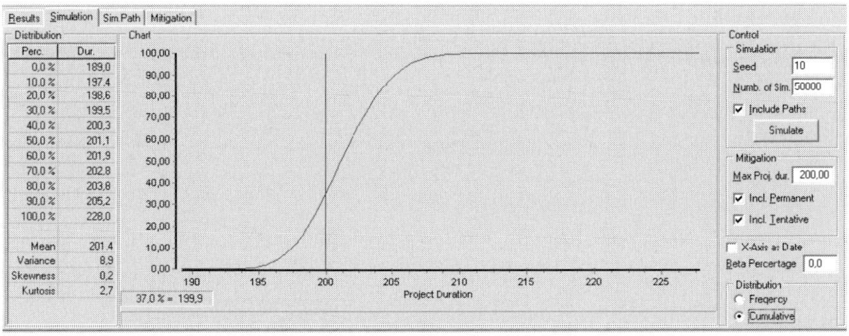

Figure C.8 Cumulative distribution function of project duration with mitigation of tasks 7 and 10.

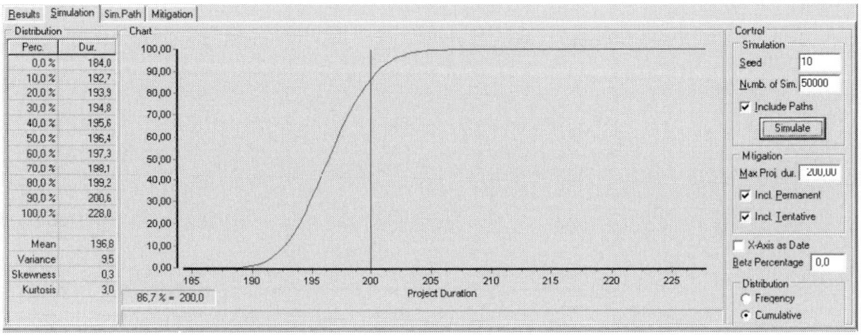

Figure C.9 Cumulative distribution function of project duration with mitigation of tasks 7, 10, 11 and 47.

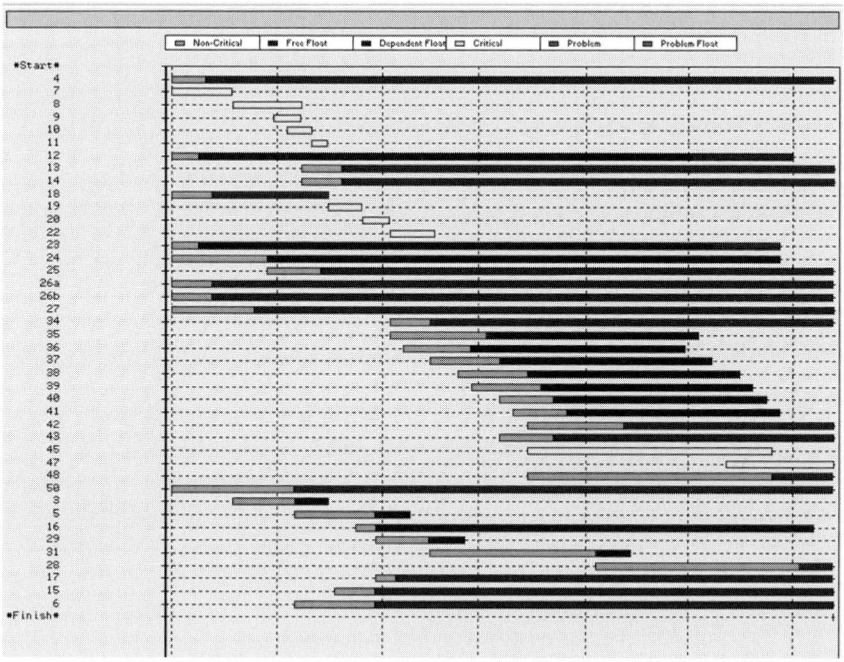

Figure C.10 Gantt chart of the project including mitigations.

C.4 Preference measurement

In this section the decision-making on the design alternatives will be discussed. With alternatives is meant: the project as designed, the project without the retail/dwelling strip or no project. The decision-making will be simulated with the Tetra tool.

A lot has been said about the decision-making on the project Nieuw Zaailand. This report will not elaborate on all the political issues that are discussed. The referendum formed a large part of these political issues. An evaluation of this referendum is made by the Universiteit Twente. In this report only the facts of the decision-making are used to simulate this process.

Groups of actors

Because in this decision-making there are no clear criteria, but there are clearly different stakeholder groups, each different stakeholder group will form a criterion. These groups are: the people that voted in the referendum, the council of the municipality, the people that did not vote in the referendum, the economic actors (developers, shop owners, etc.) and the Fries Museum.

People that voted on the referendum (A)

There were two questions posed in the referendum:

1. Are you for or against the project Nieuw Zaailand?
   (a) For.
   (b) Against.
2. Suppose the project has a majority, which alternative would have your preference?
   (a) Variant with strip.
   (b) Variant without strip.
   (c) No preference.
   (d) No variant, I am against the project.

Of course, the last answer is a strange one, because in the question is assumed that the project would be realised. Discussion about this can also be read in the evaluation of the Universiteit Twente[10].

The result of the first question was:

(a) 38%, (b) 62%.

For this report the results of the second question will be used. The result of the referendum on the second question is as follows:

(a) 31%, (b) 14%, (c) 4%, (d) 51%.

Important to note is that if option (d) was not available, most of the people would have voted for option (b). The attendance of the referendum was 43%.

The council of the municipality (B)

In the council, only 19 members were in favour of the project, while 18 were against it.

Assumption: all members of the council that voted in favour of the project, are in favour of the variant with strip and the members against the project are in favour of the variant without the strip.

The people that did not vote on the referendum (C)

In the evaluation report a research is also done on the opinion of the non-voters. The result of this inquiry was as follows:

(a) 30%, (b) 15%, (c) 20%, (d) 35%.

So, of the non-voters a lot of more people were in favour of the project.

Table C.2 Scoring of the variants.

Group	+/-	Variant within strip	Variant without strip	No project	Weight (within group)
A	+	1	2/3	0	38/100
	-	0	1/3	1	62/100
B	+	1	2/3	0	19/37
	-	0	1/3	1	18/37
C	+	1	2/3	0	65/100
	-	0	1/3	1	35/100
D	+	1	2/3	0	1
	-	-	-	-	0
E	+	1	1	0	1
	-	-	-	-	0

The economic actors (D)

In the decision-making, also the stake of the economic actors is important. These will also be united in one group. These actors are the future owners of the shops, the real estate developers, the future owners of the dwellings, etc.

Assumption: The 'economical actors' are all in favour of the project and in favour of the variant with strip.

The Fries Museum (E)

The last group that has to be taken into account is the Fries Museum. Of course they are in favour of the project. The question whether they are in favour of the strip or not, is not clear.

Assumption: The Fries Museum is in favour of the project and has no preference on variants.

Preferences and weights

All preferences are summarised in Table C.2. In this table '1' means the best that can happen, '0' is the worst option. All groups will be split up into 'pro'(+) and 'con'(-), because the order of alternatives will differ between these groups. These subgroups all have a weight within their group, which is given in the last column of Table C.2.

Assumption: People that think the variant with strip is the best score the variant without strip at 2/3 on a scale of 0 to 1, and people that think there should be no project score the variant without strip at 1/3.

Table C.3 Weighting of the groups.

Group	+/-	Weight	Weight (ff1)
A	+	38/200	0.0475
	-	62/200	0.0775
B	+	19/37	0.1284
	-	18/37	0.1216
C	+	65/200	0.0813
	-	35/200	0.0438
D	+	1	0.25
	-	0	0
E	+	1	0.25
	-	0	0

This assumption clearly is a simplification of the results of the referendum and the inquiry. Because of the difficult phrasing of the questions this information is not supplied by the results.

The only thing needed before this information can be analysed by the Tetra tool, is the weights between the different groups. Of course, this is a purely subjective value; each person would value this differently. One could say that the council represents the citizens, so the citizens need no voice. One could say that the 'non-voters' should have come to the referendum and therefore have no vote. One could say the opinion of the Fries Museum is based on a secret legacy, which will not be disclosed and therefore is not relevant. One could think the impulse to the economy is very important, so the economic actors should have a large vote. Etcetera.

For now, all groups get one vote, with the exception of group A and C; they get each half a vote[11]. In that way there are four votes: the citizens, the council, the economic actors and the Fries Museum. It must be clear that this division can easily be changed and that the method does not depend on this division. Still it is important that the division is made before the Tetra tool is used, because the division should not be a matter of political games[12]. The resulting weights are presented in Table C.3.

When these weights are imported in Tetra (by hand) all information is rounded to full percentages. A screenshot of the Tetra program with the weighting of the groups is shown in Figure C.11. Figure C.12 shows a screenshot of the scoring of the alternatives by group A.

Tetra tool results

With all the information inserted into Tetra, the tool can calculate the result. The result is shown in Figure C.13.

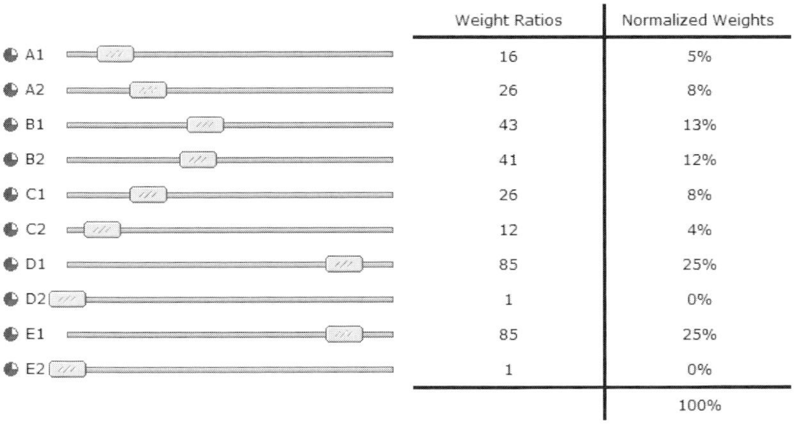

Figure C.11 Importing weights in Tetra.

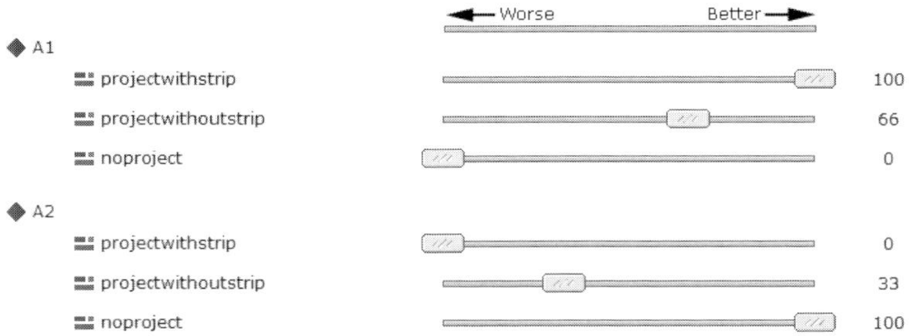

Figure C.12 Scoring alternatives in Tetra.

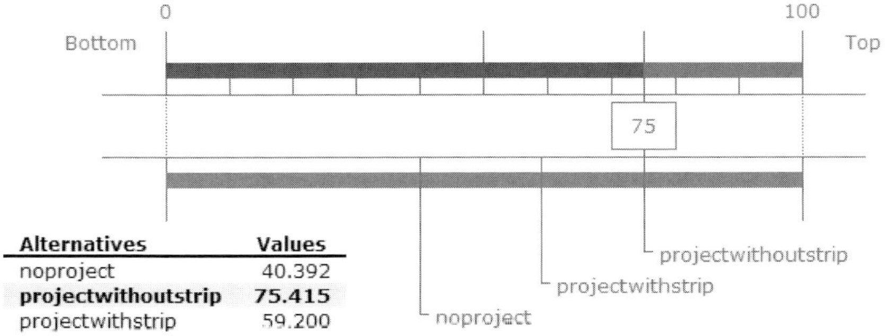

Figure C.13 Results of Tetra.

Conclusions

As can be seen in Figure C.13, the Tetra tool calculated the variant without strip as the best variant. No project is seen as the worst variant. If the council would agree with the division of the votes (one for the council, one for the citizens, one for the economical actors and one for the Fries Museum), they did a good job by deciding that the project should continue. But, according to the results they did not do the best job, because they should have chosen for the alternative without strip, as probably most stakeholders' wishes would be met. Of course this result is fully dependant on the choice of the division of the votes and the exact preference of the stakeholders. Though it is shown that this is a useful tool for such decision-making problems.

C.5 Conclusions

In this report the Open Design method is simulated on the Nieuw Zaailand project. This is mainly done on three issues: the management style, the planning, and the decision-making procedure. Each section is ended with conclusions. These conclusions will be repeated here.

Management style

PI management can be an effective way of management. This style has a lot of speed and projects can be realised sooner. Unfortunately, this management style leads more often to appeals or problems with changing goals, which in the end lead to delays. PII management is a way of project management that could be more efficient, because all stakes are involved and no power games are played. This needs a lot of investment in the beginning of the project (time and money).

It is hard to find a balance in this trade-off between getting to your goal as fast as possible and investing in the beginning of the project in the right goal. A project manager should always consider both management styles.

Cooperation between parties should be built on trust rather than on contracts and rules. A lot of time is spent (lost) on the 'development agreement', getting all the cooperation rules on paper, while it might be more efficient to build on trust. Of course, this is easier said than done. The theory of Open Design does not give enough help here.

A lot of knowledge is lost when design and realisation are separated. There could be something to gain in involving a contractor in the design phase, because of the difficult inner-city problems and the strict deadline. European regulations should not be a boundary for this.

Planning

With the Open Design tool one can simulate the project, including the chances that a task takes longer or shorter, and see how often certain mitigations are used to realise the project within time. A project manager then knows which mitigations he can take for sure and which mitigations are very effective and should be taken into account.

Preference measurement

In the simulation with the Tetra tool the variant without strip came out as the best variant. Of course this result is fully dependant on the choice of the division of the votes and the exact preference of the stakeholders (in this research assumptions had to be made).

The research did show that this is a useful tool for complicated decision-making problems in which a lot of opinions have to be taken into account.

Notes

[1]This section is based on an interview with Arthur Suiker (IPMMC), project manager of Fries Museum, in February 2009.

[2]Henket & Partners Architecten (2004), *Aanzet tot Masterplan Nieuw Zaailand.*

[3]This means that IPMMC develops the full museum project, but will not invest itself.

[4]Binnekamp, Van Gunsteren, Van Loon (2006), *Open Design, a Stakeholder-oriented Approach in Architecture, Urban Planning and Project Management*, IOS Press, Amsterdam.

[5]The solution space is determined by the constraints, which all have one owner. The municipality is the 'owner' of the constraint that the development of the public space must be of a certain quality.

[6]MSP software: *Precedence Diagram Method* version 6.10β Educational, De Graaf (2007).

[7]The exceptions and mitigations in this section are based on discussions with Arthur Suiker (IPMMC), project manager of Fries Museum, in March 2009.

[8]Within time is somewhat the same as a duration of 200 weeks. The most important deadline for this project is that task 45 is finished before 31 October 2010, but as this constraint is not supported in the software, a maximum project duration of 200 weeks was used. A consequence of this is that instead of task 45, task 47 is on the critical path.

[9]All mitigations are permanent as the software reacted strangely to tentative mitigations.

[10]Rosema (2006), *De stemming in Leeuwarden, Evaluatie van het referendum op 24 mei 2006 over het project Nieuw Zaailand.*

[11]It would be even better if the voters got 0.43 votes and the non-voters 0.57 votes, but that effect will be small, because both groups are still divided into pro and con.

[12]If the results are presented and discussion on the division of weights is still possible, one could try to influence the division in this discussion. In that way the results are steered by political power and that is not the intention of the tool.

Bibliography

Barzilai, J. (2010). 'Preference Function Modeling: The Mathematical Foundations of Decision Theory'. In Ehrgott, M., J. R. Figueira, and S. Greco (Editors), *Trends in Multiple Criteria Decision Analysis*, pp. 57–86. Springer.

Bennet, J. (1991). *International Construction Project Management*. Butterworth Heineman, Oxford.

Berends, T. C. (2007). *Contracting Economics of Large Engineering and Construction Projects*. PhD dissertation, Delft University of Technology.

Berends, T. C. and J. S. Dhillon (2004). 'An analysis of contract cost phasing on engineering and construction projects'. *The Engineering Economist*, 49(4), pp. 327–337.

Binnekamp, R. (2010). *Preference-Based Design in Architecture*. PhD dissertation, Delft University of Technology. Published by IOS Press, Amsterdam.

Binnekamp, R., L. A. van Gunsteren, and P. P. van Loon (2006). *Open Design, a Stakeholder-oriented Approach in Architecture, Urban Planning, and Project Management*. IOSPress, Amsterdam.

Blake, S. P. (1978). *Managing for Responsive Research and Development*. Freeman and Company.

Drucker, P. F. (1977). 'How to manage your boss.' *Management Review*, 66(5), pp. 9–12.

de Graaf, R. P. and L. A. van Gunsteren (2009). 'Incorporation of Mitigations on the Run in Probabilistic Network Planning'. In *EUROPIA12 2009 Conference*. Paris.

Gray, C. and W. Hughes (2001). *Building Design Management*. Butterworth Heineman, Oxford.

Van Gunsteren, L. A. (1988). 'Information Technology, a Managerial Perspective'. In Pennings, J. M. and A. Buitendam (Editors), *New Technology as Organisational Innovation*, pp. pp. 277–289. Ballinger Publishing Company, Cambridge Mass.

——— (2003). *Management of Industrial R&D, a viewpoint from practice*. Eburon Publishers, Delft, third revised edition.

Van Gunsteren, L. A. and P. P. Van Loon (2000). *Open Design, A Collaborative Approach to Architecture*. Eburon, Delft.

Hargitay, S. E. and S.-M. Yu (1993). *Property Investment Decisions, a quantitative approach*. E & FN SPON, London.

Heerkens, G. R. (2001). *Project Management*. McGraw Hill.

Hofstede, G. (2001). *Culture's consequences: comparing values, behaviors, institutions and organizations across nations*. Sage Publications, Thousand Oaks. 2nd ed.

Kerzner, H. (1998). *Project Management, a systems approach to planning, scheduling and controlling*. John Wiley & Sons, New York.

Lanza, R. B. (2003). 'Getting to Realistic Estimates and Project Plans - A Monte Carlo approach'.
URL http://www.richlanza.com/aboutrich/articles/monte.pdf

Leach, L. P. (2000). *Critical Chain Project Management*. Artech House Publishers, Boston - London.

Van Loon, P. P. (1998). *Interorganisational Design, a new approach to team design in architecture and urban planning*. PhD dissertation, Delft University of Technology, Faculty of Architecture.

Meredith, J. R. and S. J. Mantel (2006). *Project Management: a Managerial Approach*. Wiley, Hoboken.

Mintzberg, H. (1979). *The Structuring of Organizations*. Prentice-Hall, New York.

Nicholas, J. M. (2004). *Project Management for Business and Engineering*. Elsevier, Oxford.

Render, B., J. R. M. Stair, and N. Balakrishnan (2003). *Managerial Decision Modelling with Spread Sheets*. Prentice-Hall, Inc., Upper Saddle River, New Jersey.

Ritz, G. (1993). *Total Construction Management*. McGraw Hill Publishing, Maidenhead.

Van Rossem, V. (1996). *The art of city building: urban space as an architectural problem. Rob Krier in The Hague: The Resident*. NAi Publishers, Rotterdam. In Dutch.

Sneekes, J. (2003). *Kennismanagement in de bouw. Leren van ervaringen en van klanten*. Master's thesis, Delft University of Technology, Delft. In Dutch.

Twiss, B. (1992). *Managing Technological Innovation*. Pitman.

Vose, D. (2000). *Quantitative Risk Analysis: a Guide to Monte Carlo Simulation Modelling*. Wiley, Chichester.

Wijnen, G., W. Renes, and P. Storm (2007). *Projectmatig werken*. Spectrum, Houten. In Dutch, First edition 1984.

Winch, G. M. (2002). *Managing Construction Projects*. Blackwell Publishing, Upper Saddle River, New Jersey.

De Wit, T. and A. Lentjes (1998). *Damco Scheepvaart Maatschappij*. Lentjes & De Wit Maritieme Producties, Zundert.

Index

About the Author

Lex A. van Gunsteren (1938) is a business consultant, lecturer and innovator in marine propulsion. He graduated as a naval architect and received his PhD from Delft University of Technology, where in 1981 he was also appointed as Professor in Management of Technological Innovation. He was one of the pioneers of the Rotterdam School of Management where he taught management of innovation and crisis management.

After his military service as an officer in the ship design unit of the Royal Navy, he was employed, initially as an industrial scientist and later as managing director, by several technology-based companies (Lips Propeller Works, IHC Holland) and as director of corporate planning and R&D by a leading dredging and construction corporation (Royal Boskalis Westminster Group). In the late eighties, he founded an innovation company (Van Gunsteren & Gelling Marine Propulsion Development BV) for the further development of his invention of the slotted nozzle, which ultimately led to the successful applications of the so-called wing nozzle. He served on various boards and committees for monitoring R&D subsidies, among others as vice-chairman of the board of the Dutch Foundation for Technical Sciences 'STW'. Since 1997, he lectures in computer aided decision support in architecture and urban planning at the Faculty of Architecture of Delft University of Technology. His publications include six patents and eight books.